Mary Norton

Twayne's English Authors Series

Lois Kuznets, Editor
San Diego State University

TEAS 508

MARY NORTON.
Photo by Angus McBean by permission of Harcourt, Brace and Company

Mary Norton

Jon C. Stott

University of Alberta

Twayne Publishers • **New York**
Maxwell Macmillan Canada • Toronto
Maxwell Macmillan International • New York Oxford Singapore Sydney

Mary Norton
Jon C. Stott

Twayne Publishers
Macmillan Publishing Company
866 Third Avenue
New York, New York 10022

Maxwell Macmillan Canada, Inc.
1200 Eglinton Avenue East
Suite 200
Don Mills, Ontario M3C 3N1

Library of Congress Cataloging-in-Publication Data

Stott, Jon C.
Mary Norton / Jon C. Stott.
p.   cm.—(Twayne's English authors series; TEAS 508)
Includes bibliographical references and index.
ISBN 0-8057-7054-2
1. Norton, Mary—Criticism and interpretation. 2. Children's stories, English—
History and criticism I. Title. II. Series.
PR6027.0535S76 1994
823'.914—dc20   93-27319
                                                                                  CIP

The paper used in this publication meets the minimum requirements of American
National Standard for Information Sciences. Permanence of Paper for Printed Library
Materials, ANSI Z39.48-1984. ∞

10 9 8 7 6 5 4 3 2 1

Printed in the United States of America.

For Andrew and Clare and in memory of Carol and Art

Contents

Preface

To place the names William Faulkner and Peter Falk at the beginning of a preface about the English children's author Mary Norton may appear unusual, yet the American author and actor, respectively, relate to my initial response to the novels of Mary Norton and my later interest in studying her books in detail. A specialist in American literature, I first read *The Borrowers* in 1973, shortly after I had begun to teach children's literature, and was struck by the similarities between the narrative techniques of Norton's novel and those of Faulkner's *Absalom, Absalom!* Just as two Harvard roommates create a hypothetical biography about a long-dead character they have never met, so Kate and Mrs. May, in the concluding chapter of *The Borrowers,* make up a narrative about events occurring nearly half a century earlier to the Clock family, which neither of them had met. Perception of the parallels between the two novels increased my understanding of and respect for *The Borrowers.* I wrote a short article about the relationships between narrative point of view and theme in the novel and taught it several times over the next four or five years.

Then, during the 1980s, as my interests turned to other areas of children's literature, I stopped teaching *The Borrowers,* replacing it with other novels, and thought about it little, if at all. But in 1988, after my family had virtually forced me to watch a video of *The Princess Bride,* starring Peter Falk, I began to think about the Borrowers series of books again. In fact, as I watched Peter Falk playing a grandfather who tells the story of a medieval knight to his at first uninterested and then increasingly involved grandson, I began remembering Kate and Mrs. May, and especially Kate's anger when she believed that Mrs. May was going to stop telling her story at a most inappropriate point in the adventure. The video over, I went to my study and spent the rest of the evening and an hour or two past midnight reading and rereading the narrative frameworks of the first three Borrowers novels. Over the next few days, I reread the five books of the series, finding them to be not just as good as, but even better than, I had remembered.

During the eight or so years between my periods of reading and thinking about Mary Norton's books, I had been studying a number of the critical theories that had become fashionable since the late 1970s, two decades after the first four Borrowers books had been written. What I noticed in returning to the novels was how appropriate several of these critical/theoretical approaches—particularly feminist criticism, narratology, and reader response theory—were for the study of Mary Norton's work, and that they in fact helped me in perceiving dimensions of the novels I had not noticed earlier. Mary Norton was not just the creator of exciting plots and engaging characters; she was an author who sensitively examined, among other things, the nature of female development to maturity and the importance of storytelling, particularly the creative, interactive relationship between teller and listener.

Living closely with Mary Norton's eight children's novels over the next few years and gathering as much biographical information as possible, I began to think about the connections between the characters and events she created and her own life. Although she wrote about an apprentice witch, tiny people living beneath the floorboards of old country homes, and famous fairy-tale characters after the conclusion of their principal adventures, Norton seemed often to be telling her own story. Like Miss Price, the timid apprentice witch of *The Magic Bed-Knob* who postponed her training in magic until she had fulfilled family and village responsibilities, could not Mary Norton, a mother in early middle age, be seen as equally unsure as she submitted for publication the stories she had initially created for her children? Certainly, while the scenes of the Borrowers novels celebrated the Bedfordshire area in which Norton had spent a happy childhood, the portrayal of Homily's responses to her confined life before the Clocks' forced emigration and to the uncertainties of their wanderings and tenuous homes could have reflected Norton's attitudes in Portugal, far from England, isolated in the country away from the social life of Lisbon, and her own peripatetic existence during and shortly after World War II. And as a writer in her early seventies, hoping she could still engage young readers in her fictions, she must have worried, like the aging fairy-tale characters of *Are All the Giants Dead?* that she was "past it," and identified with Mildred, the writer who, in that novel, had great difficulty in getting James, the science-fiction-loving boy, to become interested in the literary world she knew best.

But if I found a lot of Mary Norton in her stories, I also found that she spoke of and about children from three different eras: those in the Borrowers series from early twentieth-century Bedfordshire, where she grew up; those of midcentury England, appearing in the frame narratives of these books and in *Bed-Knob and Broomstick,* who could have been the readers of her books when they first appeared; and children reading the books in the last decades of the twentieth century. The books do reveal the social conditions of their temporal settings. Yet even though the young people in them live in the 1910s, 1940s, 1950s, and 1970s, these characters are very similar in their personalities and in the ways they respond to events. This may well be because each reflects certain basic qualities of young people that Mary Norton finds existing in all the decades of the century. If so, it may explain her continued popularity in the 1990s, for readers still discover in the characters elements they recognize in themselves.

Mary Norton's books are consistent. While each novel is unique, certain themes, character types, and situations seem to have been of most interest to her. This study is designed to examine this unity as it is revealed in her eight novels. The first chapter not only presents biographical details but also suggests that in Norton's life are to be found many of the sources of her fictions, that all of them are in part imaginative responses to her life. Chapters 2–5 present detailed readings of the novels, applying a variety of critical approaches to close examination of the texts in order to perceive the nature and richness of the author's treatment of events, characters, and themes. Chapter 6 draws on these readings to offer a summary of Mary Norton's achievement as it relates to the personal elements of her life, the social conditions of her times, and twentieth-century British children's literature.

During the writing of this book I have received the assistance of many people. I would particularly like to thank Anne Kiefer of Twayne Publishers; my field editor, Lois Kuznets, of San Diego State University; Christine Doyle Francis of Central Connecticut University; and Raymond E. Jones of the University of Alberta. They read the manuscript at various stages of its composition and offered valuable insights and suggestions. I wish also to thank Loraine Somers, Dale Jacobs, and Jason Kapulka, my research assistants at the University of Alberta, who cheerfully and efficiently carried out innumerable tasks for me. Lynda Schultz exhibited patience far beyond the call of duty in producing innumerable printouts from a usually very confusing manuscript. All of these people have made this a better book; its defects remain my own. Finally, the dedication implies the importance of family, without which Pod, Homily, and Arriety could not have reached the end of their journey, or I the completion of this study.

Acknowledgments

Excerpts from *Are All the Giants Dead?* © 1975 Mary Norton, reprinted by permission of Harcourt Brace & Company.

Excerpts from *Bed-Knob and Broomstick*, © 1957 and renewed 1985 by Mary Norton, reprinted by permission of Harcourt Brace & Company.

Excerpts from *The Borrowers*, © 1953, 1952 by Mary Norton and renewed 1981, 1980 by Mary Norton, Beth Krush, and Joe Krush, reprinted by permission of Harcourt Brace & Company.

Excerpts from *The Borrowers Afield*, © 1955 and renewed 1983 by Mary Norton, reprinted by permission of Harcourt Brace & Company.

Excerpts from *The Borrowers Afloat*, © 1959 and renewed 1987 by Mary Norton, reprinted by permission of Harcourt Brace & Company.

Excerpts from *The Borrowers Aloft*, © 1961 and renewed 1989 by Mary Norton, reprinted by permission of Harcourt Brace & Company.

Excerpts from *The Borrowers Avenged*, © 1983 by Mary Norton, reprinted by permission of Harcourt Brace & Company.

Excerpts from *Poor Stainless, A New Story about the Borrowers*, by Mary Norton, © 1966 by Hamish Hamilton, Inc., reprinted by permission of Harcourt Brace & Company.

Chronology

1952   *The Borrowers* published in England; published in the
       United States in 1953.

1953   *The Borrowers* awarded the Carnegie Medal.

1955   *The Borrowers Afield* published in England and the
       United States.

1957   *Bed-Knob and Broomstick* published in England and the
       United States.

1959   *The Borrowers Afloat* published in England and the
       United States.

1961   *The Borrowers Aloft* published in England and the
       United States.

1970   Marries Lionel Bonsey; the couple moves to Ireland for
       several years to take advantage of that country's more
       liberal tax laws for authors.

1971   *Poor Stainless* published in England and the United
       States.

1975   *Are All the Giants Dead?* published in England and the
       United States.

1982   *The Borrowers Avenged* published in England and the
       United States.

1992   Dies 29 August 1992 in Hartland, England.

Chapter One

The Careers of Mary Norton

The writer of a biographical sketch of Mary Norton is in a position similar to that of Kate, a character in the first three books of the Borrowers series, who as an adult decides to write down for her children a story she had heard as a girl: "She wrote it all out, many years later, for her four children, and compiled it as you compile a case-history or a biographical novel from all kinds of evidence—things she remembered, things she had been told and one or two things, we had better confess it, at which she just guessed."[1] Although the facts and dates of Mary Norton's life are outlined in the Chronology, no detailed accounts of the events of her life exists. Occasional articles are based on the few interviews she gave or statements she published herself. Most of these relate the experiences of her childhood to the Borrowers books and allude briefly to her acting career, her years in Portugal before World War II, and her work and writing in England and the United States during World War II. In an article that appeared in 1982, just after publication of *The Borrowers Avenged,* she commented briefly on her activities during that period.[2] About her first marriage she is virtually silent; she mentions her four children; but she says almost nothing about her great creative period in the late 1940s and 1950s. The biographer of Mary Norton must start with dates and the author's own statements, combining them with observations of the times and places of her life and what may be autobiographical aspects of the novels themselves, and must take the advice that Kate received from Mrs. May, the old woman who had first told her about the Borrowers: "Anything we haven't experienced for ourselves sounds like a story. All we can ever do is sift the evidence" (*Afield*, 8).

Portrait of the Artist as Child, Actor, and Mother

The only daughter of Mary and Reginald Pearson, Mary Norton was born in London, England, 10 December 1903. When she was two, her father, a physician who traced his ancestry back to the famous sixteenth-century poet Edmund Spenser, moved his family to Leighton Buzzard, a small market town located 50 miles from London in southwestern

Bedfordshire. Here she spent the next six years, hiking around the countryside with her four brothers and creating stories about an imaginary race of tiny people. The period of her life about which she has written most fully, it provided much of the background for the five Borrowers books.

English life changed greatly during the years of Mary Norton's childhood. In the reign of Queen Victoria, the country had been rapidly transformed as industrialism increased, railroad lines crisscrossed the landscape, and the rich, leisured class lost much of its wealth, power, and prestige. The empire had expanded, and England had achieved great power, particularly in India, where an entire class of colonial administrators had been created. Although during the first decade of the twentieth-century many people acted as if the glorious life of the nineteenth century were as strong as ever, the country was moving toward the horrors and disillusionments of World War I.

While Mary Norton would not have been aware of the changes occurring around her at that time, she certainly seems to have been so when she came to write her children's novels. In *The Borrowers,* Great-Aunt Sophy, dreaming of wonderful times gone by, a cook, and a gardener are all who live at the once socially active Firbank Hall; the Clock family are the only remaining members of a large society of Borrowers. A branch of the human family lives in India, where one of its members will die in military duty. Mr. Pott, a character in one of the later Borrowers books, loses his leg in a railway accident, while another, Mr. Platter, builds mass-produced houses inferior to the old estates and cottages. The frequent moves of the Clocks in the various books reflect the breakup of settled patterns of life that was beginning during Norton's childhood.

Bedfordshire County, while not immune to these changes, would have seemed quiet to the young Mary, living in an old Georgian house with its huge rooms, many servants, and large grounds. The economy of the area, as one historian has noted, "was predominantly agricultural up to and beyond the turn of the century."[3] When Mary Norton learned about the world beyond the old estate she may well have reacted as did Arrietty, who, in *The Borrowers*, "stared . . . with frightened eyes"[4] when the boy told her about the world he had seen: "He told her about railway stations and football matches and racecourses and royal processions and Albert Hall concerts. He told her about India and China and North America and the British Commonwealth. He told her about July sales. 'Not hundreds,' he said, 'but thousands and millions and billions and trillions of great, big, enormous people'" (*Borrowers,* 86). To visualize more fully the scenes in which Mary Norton grew up—the drawing room, nursery, great hall, gardens, river, surrounding fields, and local village—it is best to read the descriptions in the Borrowers books, for writing from Bedfordshire to groups of American children about her novels, Norton said, "I am in the house on which much of this story was based: I did not realize how much until I arrived here some days ago."[5]

Three aspects of her childhood had a great influence on Mary Norton's writings: her shortsightedness, her tomboyishness, and her vivid imagination: "I think the first idea—or first feeling—of the Borrowers came through my being short-sighted: when others saw the far hills, the distant woods, the soaring pheasant, I, as a child, would turn sideways to the close bank, the tree roots, and the tangled grasses."[6] Later, when her condition was diagnosed, she received her first pair of glasses: "Magic. The girls on the far side of the long classroom had faces suddenly: the trees outside the window had separate leaves."[7] The adult writer's detailed, almost microscopic descriptions of objects perceived by her heroine, Arrietty, as well as the descriptions of the vast expanses of fields and villages the Clocks later saw while traveling outdoors, parallel the author's own changing visual perception of the world around her.

She was, as she called herself, the "naughty Miss Mary,"[8] a tomboy walking through fields with her brothers and a trial to the family nurse. She was sent briefly to a small Anglican convent run by two nuns and then for seven years to St. Margaret's Convent in East Grimstead, Sussex. Arrietty's rebelliousness and love of the outdoors seem to have been based in part on the author's memories of her childhood. Later, as a mother who had raised four children, she doubtless understood the frustrations experienced by Aunt Beatrice, caring for her niece and nephews in *The Magic Bed-Knob,* and Mrs. Driver, caring for the boy in *The Borrowers.*

Mary Norton led a richly imaginative life as a child, and it is about this that she has commented most often. Trailing behind her brothers on outdoor excursions, she frequently daydreamed: "Moss, fern-stalks, sorrel stems, created the *mise en scéne* for a jungle drama. . . . But one invented the characters—small, fearful people picking their way through the miniature undergrowth" (Crouch 1967, 68). She would wonder how those tiny beings, who became the Borrowers of her novels, would cope with objects and animals that, although small to human beings, were huge to them. Indoors, on rainy days or during periods of illness, she would imagine their working their way through the house and utilizing the small objects they found. She and her brothers frequently performed plays, creating their own entertainments in an era without radio, movies, television, or videotapes.

Although Mary Norton has said little about her time in the convents, she no doubt found life there tedious and confined. The only picture of a school in her novels is an unflattering one. In *The Borrowers Afield,* Kate and Mrs. May are disappointed when they discover that Firbank Hall, like the home Norton lived in, has been transformed into a drab boarding school. One aspect of her school life is significant. She recalled that "there was little time for the Borrowers, who . . . slid quietly back to the past" (*Omnibus,* ix). One is reminded of Kate's situation at the beginning of *The Borrowers Afield,* a year after she had heard the story of the Clock family: "the story of the borrowers became pushed away in the back of Kate's mind with other childish fantasies" (*Afield,* 5).

Norton's childhood was spent in an era often referred to as the "Golden Age of Children's Literature." She has not commented about her reading, but it seems highly likely that she knew the stories that were extremely popular at the time. Echoes of the fairy tales collected by the Grimm Brothers, Hans Christian Andersen, Joseph Jacobs, and Andrew Lang, particularly those dealing with the adventures of little people and giants, are found in her novels. *Are All the Giants Dead?* makes specific references to a number of stories, and the Borrowers books are filled with references to fairies. The popular books of E. Nesbit, published at the turn of the century and recounting the fantasy adventures of ordinary children, are similar to the episodes in *The Magic Bed-Knob* and *Bonfires and Broomsticks,* Norton's first two books. Arrietty's escape from her old home in *The Borrowers* and the outdoor adventures of *The Borrowers Afloat* are similar to those of Mole in Kenneth Grahame's *The Wind in the Willows* (1908). Like Mary Lennox in Frances Hodgson Burnett's *The Secret Garden* (1911), the boy in *The Borrowers* recovers his health and develops new friendships after coming to England from India. Spiller, the wild Borrower who appears in many of the Borrowers books, resembles Peter Pan, the title character of J. M. Barrie's classic of 1911.

After her years at the convent school, Norton traveled in Europe before returning to live with her family, now residing in Lambeth, a London suburb on the south side of the Thames River. Lambeth was the location of the famous Old Vic Theatre, where Norton was soon to realize what she later called "My first love (and perhaps, still, my last) . . .

the theatre."[9] Her entry into the world of the theater came when Arthur Rose, a family friend, producer of revues, and pantomime actor, visited her home for dinner: "I found, at last, the courage to say I wanted to act. 'Why not?' he said quickly, before my parents could protest. If I could learn, say, two well-known speeches from Shakespeare and recite them to him, he could gauge my chances in a flash."[10] Having prepared a speech made by Juliet in *Romeo and Juliet* and Portia's speech to Shylock about mercy from *The Merchant of Venice*, Norton went to the theatre where Rose directed: "Sometimes he would turn from a stage full of high-kicking girls and make me do my piece in the centre aisle. 'Never mind, dear, if you can do it here, you can do it anywhere.' If there came a pause in the song from the stage, I would hear my own voice ring out with shaky reference to 'bloody Tybalt' festering in his shroud" (Smaridge, 10). With Rose's help, she auditioned at the Old Vic and was accepted, first as a student and then as a paid actress.

In a book published in 1926, the Old Vic Theatre was described as standing "for Shakespeare and opera made interesting to the man in the street; for poetry and music offered at a price that the man in the street can afford."[11] Located far from London's fashionable West End theatre district, it was in "the center of a slummy, sleazy, Cockney quarter long notorious for its street-market, prostitutes, pickpockets, and specialists in more violent trades."[12] Managed by Lilian Baylis, who has been variously described as gruff, demanding, frugal, frumpy, and religious, it had been famous since 1914 for its production of both the better- and the lesser-known Shakespeare plays. The period in which Norton acted, 1925–26, was one of the theater's most successful: record-breaking crowds came to see Edith Evans, destined to become one of the most famous Shakespearean actresses of all time, perform in her first season with the company.

Years later, after she had become a renowned children's author, Mary Norton looked back fondly on this period of her life:

It still seems . . . two of the happiest years of one's life. Not always care-free, but entirely satisfying: we were privileged to act with great stars and to understudy them. I remember the first time I "played my understudy" (Bianca to Edith Evans' Katherine in *The Taming of the Shrew*)—the terror and the triumph! Then "Beauty" in *Everyman;* then "The Young Girl" in *Thirty Minutes in the Street*. . . . And so on, gradually finding one's feet and emerging from that nameless, background group called "Ladies of the Court."

How keen we were! Above the wash basin in our dressing room, someone had penned the inspiring slogan: "If the sacred fire burns in you, you will succeed. Sarah Bernhardt." And the sacred fire, at that time, burned quite as brightly as those remembered fires in the bedrooms back home [where she, her brother, and her friends had staged plays]. (de Montreville, 212)

Although Norton was to return to acting in the 1940s, the experiences of these earlier years seem to have had the most influence on her life and writing. It is tempting to see in her "daring" request to Arthur Rose at the dinner table parallels to Arrietty's initiating conversations with Tom Goodenough in *The Borrowers Afield* and Miss Menzies in *The Borrowers Aloft*. For a writer whose most famous characters would be commoners rather than aristocrats, the working-class atmosphere surrounding the Old Vic would have been a congenial one. In her function as understudy to actresses who had achieved success, Norton is not unlike her main heroine, Arrietty, a girl who, among other things, learns from two female adult role models, her mother and Miss Menzies. Certainly, the physical layout of the stage and the blocking out of scenes influenced her, as at least one critic has noted (Smaridge, 81). Many of the central episodes in Norton's novels are like dramatic scenes, usually with two or three characters interacting in an indoor or a confined/limited set. The vastness of the area about and above the stage is not unlike the shadowy interior of the clock Arrietty looks up at in *The Borrowers,* the spaces between the walls the Clock family climbs up into in *The Borrowers Afield,* the Platters' attic room in *The Borrowers Aloft,* and the enclosed fireplace in which they make their home in *The Borrowers Avenged.* In *The Borrowers Afield,* Norton specifically compares the setting to a theater: "Arrietty wandered out to the dim-lit platform; this, with its dust and shadows—had she known of such things—was something like going backstage" (*Afield,* 212).

In 1927, Mary Norton married Robert Norton, a member of a wealthy shipowning and trading family that had resided in Portugal since the Napoleonic era of the early nineteenth century. Until the outbreak of World War II in 1939, Robert and Mary lived in an old house in the isolated countryside between the towns of Cintra and Cascais, located near the Atlantic coast, 30 miles northwest of Lisbon. Here she raised her four children, Ann Mary, Robert George, Guy, and Caroline. As the effects of the Great Depression of 1929 spread from America to Europe, the family business gradually slid into bankruptcy. Mary Norton returned with her children to England after the war began, while her husband worked for the British Embassy in Portugal and then enlisted as a gunner in the British Royal Navy.

Portugal had been a maritime nation for centuries, trading with European countries and establishing colonies and trading links around the world. In his book *Portugal: The Country and Its People,* John Eppstein notes, "The call of the sea has been the main geographical factor determining the political history of Portugal."[13] A conservative Roman Catholic country emphasizing traditional family and religious values, it was "essentially a nation of poor peasants with a small and wealthy aristocracy" (Eppstein, 73). Three failed military coups had occurred in the year before the success of the Generals' National Revolution in 1926. Frequent unsuccessful revolts occurred before 1934, when a new constitution severely limited democratic freedoms.

About these 15 years of her life, Norton has said very little. Her comments, however, are interesting for the readers of her novels: "We were very cut off . . . as the roads were so bad (no government staying in power long enough to repair them) that it was a little world—with its home farm, smithy, stone mason, etc., and miles of pinewoods and cork trees. There was a man, I remember, whose only job was to paint shutters and when he reached the point at which he had started, it was time to go round again. . . . We lived an isolated life, but it was a paradise for the children" (Smaridge, 81). It was here Norton first began to write, "partly for my children" (de Montreville, 212). Coming to the isolated countryside of Portugal, after the busy, exciting, and no doubt bohemian life at the Old Vic in a working-class district of London, must have been a shock to her. Perhaps her life became like Homily's as it is described in *The Borrowers,* that of an adult female living with only her husband, frequently away at work, and her daughter, in a home far from friends or relatives. As Homily, in *Poor Stainless,* told her daughter stories, so too must Norton have told stories to her children, for the entertainment of both the teller and the listeners. Like Arrietty telling stories to her young cousin Timmis in *The Borrowers Afloat,* Norton must have felt momentary escape from the problems her family faced.

Norton described the financial crash of her husband's business: "Things went very wrong with the trade and shipping . . . and we became gradually poorer. Very gradually; it was like walking into a cold sea inch by inch, staving off with tenuous hopes the still avoidable shock. When it came at last, it was almost a relief. Everything went—houses, land, cargo, ships, tugs, lighters, copper mines" (Smaridge, 81–82). One thinks of the Clock family, who, early in *The Borrowers,* realize that they must emigrate from their home in Firbank Hall, but escape at the last moment, taking with them only a few prized possessions. Mrs. May's idea, expressed early in *The Borrowers Afloat,* about Homily's feelings arriving at her relatives' home after the Clocks' forced exodus from their own dwelling—"homeless and destitute. . . . And strange relations living above who didn't know she was coming and whom she hadn't seen for years"[14]—must certainly have been based on Norton's own emotions at this period of her life.

As the political climate in Europe darkened and the aggressions of Nazi Germany increased during the late 1930s, Mary Norton began to think of her childhood imaginings about a race of tiny people: "It was only just before the 1940 war, when a change was creeping over the world as we had known it, that one thought again about the Borrowers. There were human men and women who were being forced to live (by stark and tragic necessity) the kind of lives a child had once envisaged for a race of mythical creatures. One could not help but realize . . . that the world at any time could produce its Mrs. Drivers, who in turn would summon their Rich Williams. And there we would be" (Omnibus, x). This statement, written in 1966, reveals how, when she came to write *The Borrowers* in the early 1950s, Norton drew on both youthful memories and adult reflections.

The years of World War II, 1939 to 1945, must certainly have been unsettling for Mary Norton and her family. Her husband still in Portugal, she began work in London at the British War Office. When, however, a German invasion of England appeared imminent, she moved to New York to work at the British Purchasing Commission (since rumored to be an undercover British spy agency), settled with her children in a small house in Connecticut, and began writing to earn extra money. After two years, the family returned to London, during the period of German bombing. She resumed her acting career and wrote her first children's novel, *The Magic Bed-Knob,* first published in the United States in 1943. The aerial warfare and the darkness of the blackout periods are reflected in the novel, as frequent references are made to the war, which forms a background to the children's adventures. Near the end of the war, she was blinded when a V-2 bomb exploded nearby, but regained her sight after an operation. Certainly, the constant moving, the ever-present dangers, the insecurity, and the sense of dislocation of the family are reflected in the dangers and frequent moves faced by the Clock family in the Borrowers books.

Outlining Mary Norton's life since World War II is difficult. Various sources list these places, in order, as her residences: the Chelsea district of London; Essex; West Cork, Ireland; and Bideford, England. It is reported that in 1970, she married Lionel Bonsey and that the couple moved to Ireland, attracted by that country's more liberal tax regulations for writers. Whether she was widowed or was divorced from her first husband is not known. Critics have suggested that the novels embody Norton's responses to the various social, cultural, political, and economic changes that took place in England in the two decades during which she was most active as a writer. As Norton has said virtually nothing about her personal life since World War II, these observations are at best speculative. She died 29 August 1992, at Hartland, North Devon, England.

The Literary Career of Mary Norton: 1943–82

Remembering her years in convent school, Mary Norton once remarked, "Drawing turned out to be my forté, then acting, and lastly writing."[15] It was not until she was in her forties that she turned to this last interest. Living in America during World War II, she found that her income from the British Purchasing Commission was insufficient to support herself and her four children: "It was here I began to write in grim earnest—at night, after the children were in bed—short stories, articles, translations from the Portuguese. Later I thought of writing down some of the stories I told my children. . . . [I]n 1943, [in] London again . . . I wrote during the flying-bomb period the book now called *Bed-Knob and Broomstick*" (Johnson, 1252).

Her first novel, *The Magic Bed-Knob,* published in the United States in 1943 and in England in 1945, is the story of Carey, Charles, and Paul Wilson, three children who are sent to live in the country with their aunt during the German bombing of London and who meet Miss Price, a shy village spinster who is taking correspondence lessons in witchcraft. A spell she places on a bed-knob allows the children to travel anywhere they want. With her, they visit a supposedly deserted South Seas island, are captured by cannibals, and barely escape with the help of the apprentice witch's magic. The book was a critical success: the *New York Times Book Review* stated, "This story has all the makings of [a classic],"[16] and the *Library Journal* called it a "modern masterpiece."[17] *Bonfires and Broomsticks,* a sequel, appeared in England in 1947. The Wilson children, returning to the countryside to spend another summer, learn that the bed-knob will allow them to travel in time as well as space and go to the later seventeenth century, where they meet an inept sorcerer, Emelius Jones, whom they bring into the twentieth century to meet Miss Price. Back in the seventeenth century, Emelius is sent to the stake to be burned for witchcraft. After Miss Price and the children rescue him, the two adults marry. In 1957, when the sequel was published in the United States, combined with the first book under the title *Bed-Knob and Broomstick,* the *New York Times Book Review* proclaimed it "just as good as the first."[18] English poet John Betjeman considered it "quite the best modern fairy story I have read" (Ulman, 767).

The Borrowers, considered Norton's finest work and the novel that established her reputation as one of the foremost British children's writers of the day, was published in England in 1952 and in the United States in 1953. It is the story of the Clock family—Pod, Homily, and their teenage daughter Arrietty—members of a race of tiny people who live beneath the floorboards or between the walls of old houses, borrowing food and other necessities from the human occupants. Because he has been seen by a boy, Pod announces that they must emigrate to avoid being captured or destroyed. The family delays, however; Arrietty befriends the boy, who tells her about the world beyond her home and brings wonderful gifts of dollhouse furniture for the house-proud Homily. His activities and the existence of the Clocks are discovered by Mrs. Driver, the vindictive housekeeper, who calls in an exterminator. The family barely escapes in time, aided by the boy, who hacks a hole in a grating leading from their home to the outdoors. The events are narrated many years later by the boy's sister, Mrs. May, to Kate, a young girl who becomes progressively more involved in the story. Together, the girl and the old woman speculate on what the Clock family may have done after their escape from the house.

The Borrowers quickly achieved the status of a classic on both sides of the Atlantic. British reviewers called it "a delicious piece of fantasy, light and perfect . . . as a soap bubble" and "a brilliant piece of invention" (Senick, 220). In the United States, the prestigious *Atlantic Monthly* declared that "it has an *Alice in Wonderland* quality that puts it in a class all by itself" (Senick, 220). It received the Carnegie Medal, awarded annually by the Library Association of Great Britain for "a children's book of outstanding merit written in English and first published in the United Kingdom in the preceding year."[19] Never out of print, the book was adapted as an American television special in 1973. In 1992, the

BBC produced a miniseries combining the novel and its sequel *The Borrowers Afield.*

During the next 10 years, Norton published three sequels to *The Borrowers.* In *The Borrowers Afield* (1955), Kate, visiting Firbank Hall, the location of the Clocks' home, receives Arrietty's diary from Tom Goodenough, an old gamekeeper who had met the tiny Borrower. Using the book as a starting point, she learns that what happened to the Clocks after their escape through the grating was very different from what she and Mrs. May had speculated at the end of the first book. Fleeing across the fields, they fail to find their relatives, the Hendrearys; make a temporary home in a discarded boot; befriend Spiller, a Borrower who lives alone in nature; and are captured by Mild Eye, a gypsy. Spiller and Tom Goodenough rescue the Clocks and take them to the boy's cottage for a reunion with the Hendrearys, who live between the walls. As the novel closes, Arrietty talks to Tom, making her second contact with a human being.

In *The Borrowers Afloat* (1959), the Clock family again finds itself homeless. Homily does not get along with her sister-in-law, and after Tom and his uncle close up the cottage, there is not enough food left for two families. With Spiller's aid, the three leave through a drainpipe; establish another temporary home, this time in an old kettle, and are nearly recaptured by Mild Eye. They are again rescued by Spiller, who takes them toward a new home, Little Fordham, a nearby model village. *The Borrowers Aloft* (1961) finds the family initially happy in their new surroundings. Arrietty befriends another human being, Miss Menzies, who leaves useful objects for them to "find"; Homily has a home to her liking; Pod has work that keeps him happy. The owner of a second model village, Mr. Platter, believes, however, that possession of the Clocks will ensure financial success of his enterprise and kidnaps them. After being imprisoned in the Platters' attic for the winter, the Clocks build a balloon from discarded material they find, escape through the window, and return to Little Fordham. Pod realizes their home is unsafe and insists that Arrietty never talk to another human being. With Spiller's aid, they once more begin house hunting. In an epilogue, the author announces that, as she knows nothing about their lives beyond this point, there will be no further stories about the Borrowers.

These sequels received high critical acclaim for their plausibility and for the author's careful attention to characterization and physical detail. The *Times Literary Supplement* referred to *The Borrowers Afield* as "that rare thing, an entirely successful sequel," and the *New York Times Book Review* found it "in some ways even better [than *The Borrowers*]" (Senick, 221). *The Borrowers Afloat* was called "just as good as the earlier ones" (Senick, 222). Only *The Borrowers Aloft* received somewhat qualified praise, *Publishers Weekly* judging it "somewhat more contrived . . . but . . . better than most of the season's output all the same" (Senick, 223).

Despite her statement at the end of *The Borrowers Aloft,* Mary Norton returned to the Borrowers twice. In 1971, *Poor Stainless: A New Story about the Borrowers* appeared. Homily recounts to her daughter how, during her own childhood, one of her cousins, a mischievous tease, had escaped from the confines of Firbank Hall to spend a "never-to-be-forgotten week"[20] hiding in the village candy shop. The *New York Times Book Review* summarized the book's limitations: "[The] story . . . lacks the immediacy, drama and suspense of the other books" (Senick, 224).

In 1982, to the surprise of most people, Norton, at the urging of her British editor, Vanessa Hamilton, published a fifth novel about the Clocks, *The Borrowers Avenged.* Spiller has located a new dwelling for the Clocks in a seldom used part of the rectory of the village church. The main action takes place in the church, where the Hendreary family has taken up residence. Mr. Platter, who has been searching for his vanished prisoners, sees Arrietty's cousin Timmus[21] hiding in the church's rood screen and traps him in a cupboard. When Platter and his wife break into the church that night to recover him, they are discovered and accused of robbery. During the novel, Arrietty, who has kept her promise not to talk to a human being, meets another Borrower, Peagreen, a lame poet who becomes her confidante and who helps her to achieve a fuller understanding of and appreciation for Spiller. Although the Clocks have more security than they have enjoyed since their exodus from Firbank Hall, Peagreen's remarks, which close the novel, indicate that they can never find complete security: "'Are we?' said Peagreen gently. 'Are we? Ever [safe]?'"[22] Surprised though they may have been at the book's appearance, reviewers of *The Borrowers Avenged* were enthusiastic. British critic Margery Fisher, a longtime advocate for children's reading, praised "the tremendous vitality of the new book and the immensely satisfying, subtle way the characters have developed" (Senick, 226). Another English critic, Marcus Crouch, affirmed that "on the evidence of this book, the author is at the height of her powers still" (Senick, 227).

Mary Norton published one other children's novel, *Are All the Giants Dead?* Appearing in 1975, it is the story of James, an average modern boy who is taken during the night to a land peopled by famous fairy-tale characters, most of whose adventures are behind them. Left alone by Mildred, his guide, at an inn owned by Jack-of-the-Beanstalk and Jack-the-Giant-Killer, he learns that the two aging heroes are depressed because the former is unable to grow a beanstalk that will enable the latter to climb a nearby bluff to confront the last, apparently invincible giant. James also befriends Dulcibel, the princess who fears she must marry the toad into whose well her ball has fallen. With the assistance of James, who matures during the events as he develops a deeper understanding of human nature, Dulcibel takes control of her own destiny and the two Jacks recover their sense of self-worth by working together to destroy the giant. As the novel concludes, James finds himself back in his own bedroom.

Shorter than Norton's Borrowers novels, *Are All the Giants Dead?* is interesting for its departure from a detailed look at a geographically confined, miniaturized world to a more panoramic view of a large countryside. In her review, Margery Fisher made the comparison: "How many people must have wondered what kind of book could possibly follow the tales of the Borrowers? The one that has followed is unexpected, but as brilliant, beguiling, and original as could possibly be wished" (Senick, 225). Another British critic, Margaret Meek, praised the author's style: "Mary Norton still writes some of the best dialogue ever penned for the young" (Senick, 226). The influential American review journal the *Horn Book* demurred, however, calling the novel "a disappointing addition to the author's earlier works" (Senick, 225).

Chapter Two

Harbingers of Greatness

The Magic Bed-Knob and *Bonfires and Broomsticks*

When *The Magic Bed-Knob,* Mary Norton's first children's novel, appeared in 1943, reviewers were, as noted in chapter 1, lavish in their praise. Although the publication of the first two volumes in the Borrowers series attracted greater critical acclaim, the reissue of *The Magic Bed-Knob* in 1957, along with its sequel *Bonfires and Broomsticks,* as *Bed-Knob and Broomstick* was enthusiastically received. Canadian critic Jean de Temple noted that *The Magic Bed-Knob* "unquestionably established its author as a genuine writer of comedy,"[1] while the *Times Literary Supplement* stated, "Miss Norton indisputably has genius."[2]

The Magic Bed-Knob, relatively simple and straightforward in plot, revealed Mary Norton's debt to the traditions of the family story and the story of magic created by E. Nesbit, as well as her awareness of the World War II evacuation novel. It also displayed her unique talents: careful, precise description of telling details; sympathetic understanding of the relationships between children and adults; and witty, often satiric humor. In *Bonfires and Broomsticks,* she established a pattern she later used with great success in the Borrowers books; the creation of a sequel that not only completes aspects of the plot left unfinished in the preceding book but also clarifies and expands readers' knowledge of major characters.

The Magic Bed-Knob: Tradition and the Individual Talent

The Magic Bed-Knob begins simply. Sent to Bedfordshire to live with their repressive aunt during the World War II bombing of London, Carey Wilson and her two younger brothers, Charles and Paul, learn that their prim, middle-aged spinster neighbor is an inept apprentice witch. When the children visit her laboratory, she changes Paul briefly into a frog and, to bribe the children not to divulge her secret, puts a spell on a bed knob Paul has in his pocket. When twisted, it has the power to take his bed anywhere the children wish. They depart excitedly, but return the next day announcing that the spell has not worked. This, Miss Price discovers, is because, Carey, not Paul, had twisted the knob and made the wish. That evening, after discussing possible exciting destinations, Carey and Charles give in to Paul's demand that they travel to their London home to see their mother; however, the house is closed and their mother away, and they and the bed are discovered by a policeman, who takes them to the station, where they spend the night. The next morning, the children are found missing, along with the bed, which they have wished back home. Later that day, Carey suggests that Miss Price join them on a trip to Ueepe, an apparently uninhabited South Seas island.

At first, it seems like an idyllic day-trip to the seashore: Miss Price reads her book, Paul plays with his bucket and spade, and Carey and Charles go off to swim in a freshwater pool. But as sunset approaches, the idyll turns into a nightmare. They are captured by cannibals, and Miss Price must use her magic to defeat a witch doctor in a struggle for her broom.[3] Gathering the children onto her broomstick, she flies them to the bed, where Paul wishes them home. Although they are safe in Bedfordshire, their troubles are not over. When the maid notices how wet and messy both bed and children are, Aunt Beatrice announces that the latter are to be sent back to London on the noon train. Paul and Carey say a hasty good-bye to Miss Price, who announces that she is thinking of giving up magic. As they travel unhappily home, Paul informs them that he has brought the bed-knob with him.

This brief plot outline indicates that *The Magic Bed-Knob* grows out of one firmly established and two more recent genres of British children's fiction: stories about families of ordinary children encountering magic, made popular by E. Nesbit at the beginning of the twentieth century; the stories about a gruff but kindly witch found in P. L. Travers's *Mary Poppins* (1934), *Mary Poppins Comes Back* (1935), and *Mary Poppins Opens the Door,* published in 1943, the same year as *The Magic Bed-Knob;* and the stories of children evacuated from London during World War II.

As Marcus Crouch wrote about Nesbit, "No writer for children today is free of debt to this remarkable woman. . . . [S]he managed to create the prototypes of many of the basic patterns in modern children's fiction. . . . In her 'Five Children' stories she initiated the comedy of magic applied to the commonplaces of daily life."[4] In *Five Children and It* (1902), *The Phoenix and the Carpet* (1904), and *The Story of the Amulet* (1906), Nesbit recounted the adventures of a group of children who "were not particularly handsome, nor . . . extra clever, nor extraordinarily good. But they were not bad souls on the whole; in fact, they were rather like you."[5] Through the agency of a phoenix, they are able to travel anywhere they wish on the family's new carpet, and a *psammead,* or sand fairy, shows them how to use a half-amulet to transport themselves to different periods of the past. As Mary Croxson has noted, each of Nesbit's children is portrayed as a unique individual within the family group, and all experience a kind of "healthy neglect" from adult authority figures, particularly parents, and have "an unusually free relationship with adults."[6]

Having read the title of Mary Norton's book, with its adjective *magic,* and the opening page, with its description of three average siblings on their own during vacation, the experienced child reader would probably have placed the novel in the Nesbit tradition. Awareness of the relationship between the novel and the tradition would become clearer as the reader learned of the Wilsons' acquisition of the power to travel magically and of their developing relationship with the unusual Miss Price. Nesbit's children, however, had received their magical powers from enchanted beings. Norton's receive theirs from an apprentice witch, Miss Price, who accompanies them on the second of their two trips.

The relationship between a witch and ordinary children and their growing friendship reminded many reviewers of Mary Poppins, who in P. L. Travers's enormously popular first two books about her had entered the routine lives of the four Banks children and escorted them into realms of wonder and enchantment. A crusty, middle-aged single woman, Mary Poppins was very unlike the fairy godmothers of traditional tales. Miss Price's character is in many ways different from Mary's; however, like Mary, she is neither a typical middle-aged spinster nor a fairy godmother, and also like Mary, she takes children away from the pleasant yet somewhat dull routine of their lives.

Although unnoticed by reviewers and critics, the evacuation novel was a major literary influence on wartime editions of *The Magic Bed-Knob.* During the bombings of urban centers, thousands of English children were moved to the safety of the countryside or farther afield to Ireland, South Africa, the United States, and Canada, as happened to Norton and her children, who moved to Connecticut. In addition to the trauma of leaving their families, the children had to face the not infrequent hostility of their hosts and the anxieties of wondering about relations and friends back in the cities. Adult writers such as Joyce Carey, in *Charley Is My Darling* (1940), and Henry Green, in *Loving* (1945), dealt with the theme. Several children's novels also appeared. Kitty Barne's

Visitors from London (1940), winner of the Carnegie Medal as the top British children's book of the year, projected what critics Mary Cadogan and Patricia Craig have termed "a country holiday rather than a wartime atmosphere."[7] Angela Brazil's *Five Jolly School Girls* (1941) was patriotic in tone. P. L. Travers's *I Go by Sea, I Go by Land* (1941) depicts the anxieties of a dangerous transatlantic passage to the United States.

The opening sentences of the wartime editions set *The Magic Bed-Knob* within the context of World War II and the evacuation of children. Carey, Charles, and Paul are sent to Bedfordshire "because it was not safe for them to be in London."[8] References to blackout shades and food rationing are frequent; barrage balloons and Spitfire planes pass overhead; and when Carey is awakened by the London policeman sitting on the bed, "she thought it was an air raid, with a direct hit on the bed" (*Magic,* 46). Finally, as Aunt Beatrice prepares to send them back to London, she tells the children that they must return to their mother, "war job or no war job" (*Magic,* 107). Although the main events of the story are not concerned with the children's status as evacuees, the conditions of life in wartime Britain are never too far in the background.

While *The Magic Bed-Knob* exists within literary tradition, Mary Norton does not slavishly follow conventions or imitate specific authors. The originality noticed by early reviewers arises in part from the way Norton uses and presents these conventions to tell her own, unique story. Unlike Nesbit's children, who live within a relatively safe late Victorian England, hers have been sent away from their mother because of the dangers of war, and unlike the phoenix and the *psammead,* Miss Price is an inept granter of magic boons who needs the encouragement and friendship of Carey, Charles, and Paul. Miss Price is also quite unlike the experienced, self-confident, and self-possessed Mary Poppins. While, like Travers's character, she enlivens the routines of the children and grows progressively fonder of them, Miss Price is uncertain of what role she should play in front of them, and her insecurities and rapidly shifting emotions are readily apparent.

It is tempting to argue that in many ways, Mary Norton is consciously adapting or even parodying the traditions within which she is writing. Parody, as Linda Hutcheon has demonstrated, is "imitation with critical difference."[9] Specific works or the conventions of established literary genres are used by authors who, in their own works, exaggerate, invert, or otherwise alter these recognized elements. Sometimes the object of the parodist is to draw attention to perceived inadequacies of the parodied works or conventions; more frequently, Hutcheon argues, the parody is a vehicle of satirizing "contemporary customs or practices" (Hutcheon, 11). By emphasizing the difference in their use of traditions or works, authors can use these to communicate their own visions. To achieve these purposes, "there must be certain codes shared between the encoder and the decoder" (Hutcheon, 27).

Given the popularity of Nesbit's and Travers's books, it is reasonable to assume that Norton counted on her readers' awareness of the similarities and differences between those works and *The Magic Bed-Knob*. Whereas Nesbit's magic phoenix had given the five children the ability to turn the mundane rug into an enchanted fairy-tale-type flying carpet, for the Wilsons a simple bed knob is the talisman. Although the bed does take them places, when they arrive at their destination, it remains a bed, incongruous in the London street or the sandbar of a tropical island. Whereas the Banks children watch as Mary Poppins "slid gracefully up the banisters,"[10] when Paul had first watched Miss Price, "she had wobbled so."[11] In what may be an implicit reference to Mary Poppins's use of her umbrella for catching the wind, Norton describes Miss Price's fall from her broom this way: "the broomstick came down quite slowly, like an umbrella blown inside out, with Miss Price clinging to the handle" (*Bed-Knob*, 17). But if the Wilsons' mode of conveyance or first destination is not so glamorous as those of Nesbit's characters, their adventures are equally exciting and the qualities of character they reveal equally significant. And if Miss Price is a Mary Poppins manqué, or at best an apprentice Mary Poppins, her use of magic to rescue herself and the children, given her inexperience, emphasizes her great courage. Readers who recognize the differences between Norton's book and those in the traditions can use their awareness to help them better understand her characters and their actions.

Norton does not parody the evacuation novel, but she does use the war background to enhance characterization. Little Paul's insistence that they use the magic to visit their mother and their reactions on finding her away from home imply the loneliness they all must have felt as evacuees. Because they have caused Elizabeth's resignation as maid, Aunt Beatrice puts personal feelings ahead of the war effort and returns them to London. Miss Price is not so selfish; she resists the temptation to use her magic to double her wartime butter rations. That she is upset on learning that the children are returning to ravaged London indicates the genuine fondness for them she has come to feel. Undoubtedly, Mary Norton's own children and wartime readers are found enjoyable escape in the story. Perhaps they also learned that courage, gentleness, and warm hearts such as are found in Miss Price and the Wilsons were more important during wartime England than any magic.

Mary Norton's achievement in *The Magic Bed-Knob* is to be found in more than just her original use of literary conditions and earlier works. Most early reviewers, including those who noticed the links to Nesbit and Travers, commented on her telling use of precise, concrete details, her skillful mixture of the ordinary and the magical; and her sensitive characterization of both Miss Price and the Wilson children. Interestingly, few have commented on the plot itself. Compared with Nesbit's or Travers's stories, the plot is relatively slight. By the end of the third chapter, all that has happened is that the children have discovered that Miss Price is a witch and that she has placed a charm on the bed knob. The fourth through seventh chapters present their trip to their own neighborhood and the nearby police station and their return to Bedfordshire, where they plan their tropical excursion. Only in the eighth chapter are there danger and excitement, as they are captured by the cannibals. The ninth and tenth chapters find the children back in Bedfordshire. These events are important only as they assist in characterization. Average children, visiting an uninteresting countryside, discover that their apparently ordinary neighbor is acquiring extraordinary powers that will influence them. Norton's presentation of how these events influence them and Miss Price and their interrelationships accounts for much of the novel's initial and continuing success.

With the exception of Miss Price, the children have little contact with adults. At one extreme are Aunt Beatrice and her housekeeper, Elizabeth, both of whom can be categorized as what early twentieth-century British writer Kenneth Grahame called "Olympians," grownups who "treated us . . . with kindness enough as to the needs of the flesh, but after that with indifference . . . , and therewith the commonplace conviction that your child is merely animal."[12] Elizabeth views them as at best a nuisance and inconvenience. Aunt Beatrice meets with them only at lunch in her somber dining room, or at the story's conclusion, in her study, where she stares at them, her "pink-rimmed eyes . . . like agates" (*Bed-Knob,* 90), and informs them "in her precise, cutting voice" (*Bed-Knob,* 87) that they are to be returned home. Weary and overworked, the police sergeant, inspector, and matron are kind and baffled, but seem almost relieved at the children's mysterious disappearance. The cannibals view them as objects, supplies for dinner, dropping Carey "on her head as if she were a sack of potatoes" (*Bed-Knob,* 72), and the witch doctor seems not to notice them.

The importance of Miss Price to each of the children is determined by
the characters and needs of each, by the differences between her and the
other adults they meet, and by her unique character. The possibilities for
adventure her magic affords make faint appeals to a latent adventurous-
ness in the reticent and timid Charles. Spontaneous, impish, and imaginative, Paul responds to both the excitement her magic offers and the
special status she gives to him, both of which lessen his need for his
mother and his sense of being the baby of the family. For Carey, nearing
the end of childhood, Miss Price may be like the crone figure discussed
by many feminist critics,[13] the wise old woman who helps the girl move
toward maturity. Under the influence of Miss Price, Paul, the baby,
becomes a child; Charles is able to move slightly away from his timidity;
and Carey begins to relate her concepts of fair play and compassion to
real people and situations. Like a fairy godmother, whom she little
resembles outwardly, Miss Price has helped them to develop their inner
potentials.

Of the three Wilson children, Charles, the middle child, seems to be
the least involved in the adventures. "[B]y nature extremely retiring"
(Bed-Knob, 38), he does not speak to Miss Price during their initial meeting with her, or in front of the policeman, the matron, Aunt Beatrice, or
Elizabeth. But in addition to being shy, he knows the value of silence,
kicking Paul under the table to prevent his telling about Miss Price,
knowing not to hint to Miss Price that they will swim without their
suits, and refusing to rail against the cannibal carrying him into the jungle, as Carey does. Although uncomfortable that he, Carey, and Paul are
conspicuous standing by their bed on the London street, he seems to
have a hidden longing for adventure. He admires Carey's bravery in
standing next to Miss Price, who has just revealed a trace of wickedness;
from his hiding place in the stairwell, mocks the adults who notice the
bed; twice grumbles that the trip is not very adventurous; and suggests
the South Seas, the South Pole, and Tibet as destinations. His potential
for enjoying adventure will be fulfilled in the novel's sequel, *Bonfires and
Broomsticks*. A hint of it, however, is revealed on the trip home to
London; he seems the glummest and remarks that he would use the bed-
knob, if they had it.

As the youngest in the family, Paul often feels much put upon—
"aggrieved," as the author frequently states—by his older brother and
his sister. Although at times he is treated like a baby and does not always
know what is happening, he is a strong-willed child, taking a delight in
things wicked: he is pleased when Miss Price lets her evil tendencies

show, happy that they are in prison, disappointed to learn it is only a
police station, and excited when he tells the others that the savages plan
to eat them.

Perhaps most important, because of him the children enter into the
world of magic. Long before he told Carey and Charles about Miss Price,
he had known she was a witch. He had not informed them because he
feared not being believed; because "it had been his secret, his nightly
joy" (*Bed-Knob,* 16); but most important, "because he wanted to be
proud of Miss Price" (*Bed-Knob,* 17). He produces the bed knob and is
granted the right to use the spell. At the end of the story, he is disappointed that Miss Price has rejected magic: "He had an uneasy feeling
that Miss Price was turning over a new leaf before he had finished with
the old one" (*Bed-Knob,* 93). Yet he assures Carey, as they depart for the
train station, that Miss Price will not abjure magic.

Paul's closeness to Miss Price and her magic is appropriate. As the
baby of the family, the least influential of the children, he experiences
loneliness and a sense of displacement from his mother that must be
considerable. His joy at watching Miss Price, his possession of a secret,
and his increasing pride in her provide him with happiness and a sense of
self-worth. Like the youngest sibling in many folktales, he has the greatest faith and imaginative belief of the three, and therefore the qualities
necessary to make the magic work. Carey and Charles, although they
continue to give him orders, develop a new appreciation for him because
of his important role. On being informed that Paul possesses the spell,
the others view him in a new light.

The strongest relationship exists between Carey and Miss Price. Carey
reveals her dominant traits during the early morning rescue of the
woman. She takes the lead, rushing to her; assumes command, telling
Charles to get a doctor; and is considerate, putting her arm around Miss
Price because it was appropriate behavior. She also has a strong sense of
fair play, telling Paul that he was mean for not sharing his secret about
Miss Price. Not surprisingly, Carey is the one who bravely confronts Miss
Price about her witchcraft and proposes the exchange of magic power for
the children's secrecy. At this point, her relationship with Miss Price
seems self-serving, but there are small hints that she is beginning to
admire her neighbor as a person. Learning of the magic, "she pointed out
almost reproachfully, 'you could have done that at the church concert,
instead of singing'" (*Bed-Knob,* 20).

Caught by the policeman, Carey reacts in a way that reveals both her
sense of fair play and moral obligation and a certain self-interestedness.

Asked where the bed came from, "Carey hesitated. Trouble—that was
what they were heading for. She thought again of Aunt Beatrice. And of
Miss Price—oh, Miss Price, that was the worst of all; to tell about Miss
Price would be the end of everything—yet no good ever came of lying"
(*Bed-Knob,* 42-43). The loss of the newly acquired magic would, to her,
be worse than the fact of betraying Miss Price. Carey's self-interest is also
behind the anger she directs at Paul: "I told you this was a stupid kind
of wish. I tried to warn you. . . . Miss Price will get into trouble. We shall
have broken our promise. It will be the end of the magic bed-knob. . . .
And it's Charles and me who'll get the blame" (*Bed-Knob,* 49).

The next stage of development in Carey's relationship with Miss Price
occurs the day following the trip to the police station. After noticing
that the woman is planting edelweiss, a plant supposed to grow only
above the snowline, Carey learns that Miss Price is planning to enter the
village flower show. Suspecting that the woman is using magic to gain
unfair advantage, her sense of fair play is aroused and she confronts Miss
Price with her thoughts. In an exchange that takes place while the boys
are sleeping, the older woman expounds on the unfair advantage enjoyed
by the wealthy, and explains that just because she is a witch, she cannot
produce money. Carey replies, "'I see.' And it was indeed as clear as day-
light to her" (*Bed-Knob,* 60). Norton does not provide an antecedent for
the indefinite pronoun. The implication is clear, however, that Carey has
acquired a better understanding of the limitations not only of witchcraft
but also of her notions of fair play. She begins to see Miss Price as a complex individual, not just as a neighbor or witch. Interestingly, at this
point Carey invites Miss Price to join them on the next expedition,
because she likes her and would feel safer if the woman accompanied
them. No longer the confident leader, she begins to see her limitations
and the importance of interrelationships. Miss Price is not just the person who could remove the spell from the bed knob; she is an adult
whose special help they may and, as it turns out, do need.

The confrontation with the witch doctor is described from Carey's
point of view, and her reactions indicate not just that she is thinking
about how a victory by Miss Price will lead to their escape, but that she
wants Miss Price to succeed for her own sake. "'Oh, Miss Price!' she
breathed, 'Miss Price,' as people call the name of their side at a football
match" (*Bed-Knob,* 75). The girl's observations are accompanied by
thoughts based on her knowledge of the woman's character. She remembers Miss Price's statement about worry causing her to forget the few
spells she knew by heart; is pleased when Miss Price laughs because that

indicates she is not getting fussed; and interprets Miss Price's steadfast expression as an indication of her total absorption in the task.

Whereas Carey had not wanted to tell the policeman about Miss Price for fear of losing the spell, she refuses to divulge the secret of the wet bed to her aunt out of loyalty to her friend. She had warned her brothers: "*Whatever happens, . . .* we mustn't give away Miss Price. Except for that, it doesn't matter what we say because nothing could be worse" (*Bed-Knob,* 87). Carey's disappointment in learning that Miss Price is giving up magic does not appear to be motivated by selfishness. She refers to the witch as "Darling Miss Price" (*Bed-Knob,* 93); calls her a good sport, a type of person she values highly; and hugs her warmly. This spontaneous, heartfelt gesture, when compared with her dutiful hugging of the injured Miss Price when they first met, indicates the growth of Carey's affections.

The importance of Miss Price to the children and to the novel itself is explicitly signaled in the fifth paragraph of the first chapter: "One day slipped into another, and all the days were alike—until Miss Price hurt her ankle. And that's where the story begins" (*Bed-Knob,* 11–12). The injury to Miss Price will turn an ordinary summer vacation into something unusual, interesting, and exciting—in short, into a story. It does this because it leads to the children's finding out that she is a witch, to her bestowal of the spell, and to the subsequent travels. More significant, as we have seen, Miss Price helps each of the children to grow as an individual.

In addition, Miss Price herself grows through her interaction with them. Until her meeting with the Wilson children, she has led a double life. As a member of the Bedfordshire village, she is an ordinary spinster. "You all know somebody rather like Miss Price" (*Bed-Knob,* 12) the narrator comments before describing her appearance and her mundane activities: "In all the village there was none so ladylike as Miss Price" (*Bed-Knob,* 12). Yet as she later tells Carey, "ever since I was a girl, I've had a bit of a gift for witchcraft, but somehow—what with piano lessons and looking after my mother—I never seemed to have the time to take it up seriously" (*Bed-Knob,* 19). Her small, tidy home symbolizes her life. Beyond the flower-bordered walkway and the small sitting room is her witch's laboratory, unknown to anybody but herself until the children enter it. Before Carey, Charles, and Paul come into her life, she has accomplished little with her secret talents. She is only now learning how to control her broomstick, and she finds it difficult to remember and then execute her spells successfully. The main use of her new knowledge seems to take place in her garden.

Miss Price's life is sharply divided: outwardly, she has lived according to social expectations, caring for her mother, visiting the sick, teaching piano, and deporting herself acceptably. Her obligations have forced her to repress her gift; her social standing requires that she conceal her activities: flying only at night, keeping her laboratory locked, and limiting the visible use of her magic to growing exotic plants. Her fears and her tears when she is discovered by the children are caused by her belief that they will make her witchcraft public knowledge. Her first name symbolizes her dual nature: Eglantine is a prickly but sweet-smelling rose. As its sharp thorns keep one away, so does Miss Price's reserved, distant manner. Its pleasant aroma may reflect her basic kindness and gentleness, a love of people that has been restricted to her relations with her mother and the sick. In meeting the children, her secret life, one she would like to be proud of, is revealed to outsiders. Moreover, during the course of the story she is able to display her talents and in so doing to save the children, for whom she has developed a genuine affection. The two aspects of her character come closer together by the end of the novel; in the sequel, they will be united.

The initial changes in her character are evident during the children's first two visits to her home. She is happy to have her talents recognized: when Carey remarks on her cleverness, she blushes with pleasure and has "a spot of proud pink in each cheek" (*Bed-Knob,* 27) as she shows them her workplace; she speaks with a note of triumph when she discovers that her spell on the bed knob is effective. The children offer her a chance to relate to others. Suppressing a momentary impulse of wickedness, she listens to Carey's suggestion about the exchange of a spell for secrecy, partly because the suggestion provides her with a chance to perform an experiment she had wanted to try. It is implied that the magical travel is something she has been too timid to try alone. Like an anxious parent, she twice warns the children not to get into trouble with the spell, enjoins moderation, and sends them off with the caution "Have a good time, keep to the rules, and allow for the bed" (*Bed-Knob,* 33). Her instructions reveal both her heretofore repressed maternal instincts and her own timidity.

When the children return from London, Miss Price is eager as an apprentice witch to know if the spell worked and interested as an adult in the children's experiences, hoping they had a good time. When Carey invites her to accompany them on the South Seas trip, she is fussed, but happy that she has been included: she may be able to gather another exotic plant, and she will enjoy the change. But she also tells Carey that she wishes the trip to be more orderly than the first one and arrives prepared with picnic lunch, book, umbrella, dark glasses, and her father's army sun helmet. The proper village lady will take a magic trip in the manner of an adult taking children for a day excursion to the seashore. She can be both a decorous chaperone and an enchantress. One item in her inventory reveals an important aspect of her character. Looking over her shoulder at her book, Paul reads a chapter title aloud: "Another Man's Wife" (*Bed-Knob,* 67). Lonely Miss Price seeks love vicariously.

In her confrontation with the witch doctor, Miss Price achieves many victories. The sorcerers' duel is not something she has entered into just to prove herself to herself and others; it is a mortal struggle, with the lives of her friends at stake. Whereas turning Paul into a toad during the children's first visit had been a simple demonstration of a simple spell, performing it on the witch doctor in a life-and-death situation is no mean feat. In her combat against a formidable opponent, she maintains an impassive face, concealing her emotions as she had been unable to do in early meetings with the children. As she flies the children away from the savages' encampment, she makes more masterful use of the broomstick than she has ever done before. Finally, it is a public struggle, albeit on an isolated tropical island. The public doer of good deeds has exhibited heretofore hidden talents that far exceed anything she has done before, and she has done so to save her friends.

When the group returns to the children's bedroom, Miss Price might appear to have reverted to her former self. Nervous, flustered, and incapable of initiating action, she must be motivated by Charles and Carey. When they go to say good-bye, she is in the garden, as she was after the children's first adventure; however, there is a significant difference in her response to them. Then, concern about the success of her spell was paramount; now, she is upset that the children must leave, feels responsible for this, and exhibits no relief when they tell her that her secret is safe. Moreover, she has given up her plans to use magic in the flower show, agreeing with Carey that it might be cheating. Her final words reveal the depth of her feeling for the children and her recognition of their inner strengths: "Keep your warm hearts, your gentleness, and your courage. They will do . . . just as well as magic" (*Bed-Knob,* 93). Instead of crying, as she had at first done when she feared the revelation of her secret, she exhibits now only a single tear on her nose, an indication of her deep feelings for the children.

At this point in the novel, the specific adventures are completed. The children, having moved from the uneventful vacation and into and out of fantastic adventures, are to be reunited with their mother at home in London. All have grown as a result of their experiences. Miss Price has found a sense of self-worth and developed her repressed self—not only her gift for magic but also her love for others. Miss Price and the children have mutually benefited. But although the book is neatly finished, the story is not really over. When Miss Price placed the spell on the bed knob, she had enabled it to travel in time as well as space. Paul's revelation that he has brought the bed knob back to London with him opens the possibility for a sequel involving time travel. Moreover, written as it is within a tradition that includes the works of Nesbit and Travers, *The Magic Bed-Knob* belongs to a genre that generally produces sequels. But more than the plot and the genre demands a sequel. Charles had shown little character growth and had participated little in the adventures. Miss Price had only begun to develop her hidden personality; she was still a divided person. To complete the stories of both, another novel was needed.[14] Even as *The Magic Bed-Knob* was going through the press, Norton had begun to create that sequel.

Bonfires and Broomsticks: Creating Closure

The events of *Bonfires and Broomsticks* occur two years later. "The memory of that summer became a secret thing, seldom spoken of—and never with Paul" (*Bed-Knob,* 97). He has been convinced that he dreamed the events, and Charles, busy with school, finds the events becoming unreal to him—until Carey discovers a newspaper advertisement, placed by an E. Price, offering to board children for the summer holidays. When Charles, Paul, and Carey return to Bedfordshire, bringing the magic bed-knob with them, they learn that Miss Price has bought Paul's bed from the estate of the deceased Aunt Beatrice, that the bed-knob is now missing from their luggage, and later, that Miss Price and Paul have gone into the past on the bed.

Her sense of fair play aroused, Carey confronts Miss Price and is told that the children can make one trip into the past. They travel to the Cripplegate district of London, one week before the Great Fire of 1666, where they meet Emelius Jones, an inept and timid necromancer whom they bring back to the twentieth century. Annoyed at first, Miss Price blushes when Emelius praises her skills at magic and is impressed when he describes the house he is to inherit. After he returns to the seventeenth century, Emelius is arrested and convicted of witchcraft. His hopes revive when Miss Price appears at his cell window, promising to help. The children, who have followed the large crowds moving toward the execution site, see her swooping toward the burning stake on her broomstick. When broomstick and rider crash to the ground, apparently shot by soldiers, Charles rushes to the stake, cuts Emelius's bonds, and leads him, Carey, and Paul to safety. They find Miss Price, who is unhurt and angry at the children's disobedience: she had created an effigy from her clothes, placed it on the broomstick, and willed it into the square.

Safely back in the twentieth century, the children become worried at Miss Price's increasing kindness and gentleness. They soon discover the reason: she has accepted Emelius's marriage proposal, is selling her house and most of its possessions, and will return to the seventeenth century to live in Emelius' newly inherited cottage, not far from the location of her own house. After she has departed, the children wander up the hill to the ruins of Emelius's homesite. There Carey fantasizes that she sees the happy couple entering their home. Her blissful expression changes to shock, however, when she actually hears Miss Price, her final words reaching the girl across the centuries: "Carey, come at once out of those lettuces" (*Bed-Knob,* 189).

Like the Wilson children traveling back to Bedfordshire with expectations based on their memories of their earlier summer adventures and their knowledge of Miss Price's personality, readers will begin *Bonfires and Broomsticks* with expectations of plot and characterization based on their recollections of *The Magic Bed-Knob.* As in the first book, the children leave their London home for a country summer vacation; make two major journeys on the bed, the second very dangerous; and return very quickly to their London home. The characters of Paul, Carey, Charles, and Miss Price are consistent with the traits they had earlier displayed. This, however, is no mere repetition of a plot formula, as is the case in books of the Stratemeyer Syndicate, such as the Nancy Drew or the Hardy Boys series, in which only superficial specifics of plot, secondary characters, and settings are altered. Norton's sequel requires readers to use their awareness of similarities and differences between the two books to help them understand the second. It belongs to a category of books that Roderick McGillis suggests "speak to and from each other."[15]

The plot differences between the two novels are obvious. The children initiate the second trip to Bedfordshire and stay at a different house. They travel in time, not space, and bring someone back with them. Finally, at the novel's conclusion both the children and their hostess depart, and the children no longer possess the magic bed-knob. Other differences are less immediately obvious. Although stuffed alligators are found in the laboratories described in each novel, Miss Price's neat, orderly laboratory contrasts with the dimly lit, cluttered one of Emelius. In the first book, the children are taken to a "jail" filled with kindly adults; here Emelius is cast into a dank prison to await execution. Miss Price confronts a witch doctor in a humorous duel for control of her broomstick; she engages in "intrasubstantiary-locomotion" (*Bed-Knob*, 181) in a grim attempt to rescue Emelius from the stake. Miss Price, always a careful preparer for the bed trips, takes her father's sun helmet to the tropical island, but packs his sword for the trip to the past. Charles is unhappy at being conspicuous in his pajamas and complains at having to walk barefoot to the police station; unconcerned for himself, he rushes in pajamas and robe to liberate Emelius and ignores his scorched feet as he leads his siblings and Jones from the square.

These opposites, speaking to each other between books as it were, create a sense of balance or completeness that brings the second book to a satisfying conclusion. The most important aspect of this completeness is seen in Norton's presentation of the characters' development, particularly that of Charles and Miss Price. Paul, although he still possesses the power to wish the bed to desired locations, is relatively unimportant in the novel; he seems almost to have been relegated to baby status.

On a casual reading, Carey would seem to develop little, acting basically as a catalyst in the growing romance between Miss Price and Emelius Jones. Yet the deepening of the special relationship she had established with Miss Price two summers earlier indicates her growth toward adulthood. While Charles's happiness at returning to the country is based on his anticipation of further magical adventures, Carey is simply happy to be seeing Miss Price again: "something about her long pink nose comforted Carey suddenly. It was a kind nose, a shy nose, a nose that had had a tear on the tip of it once . . . ; it was a reassuring nose; it was Miss Price. . . . Carey suddenly felt rested and happy and full of peace" (*Bed-Knob,* 107). The extent of Carey's fondness for Miss Price becomes apparent on the morning after their first trip to the past, when she announces that they have returned with Emelius Jones. In his lodgings, Carey is sensitive to Emelius's timidity and sense of abjectness, and on discovering that, despite his appearance, he is only 35 years old, asks, "Have you had a sad life?" (*Bed-Knob,* 133). Learning that he is from Bedfordshire, she wishes aloud that he could see it in the twentieth century, and along with the other children, indirectly speaks about Miss Price. Sympathetic to both adults and perceiving the interests they share, Carey is playing the role of matchmaker. When she brings

Emelius to the breakfast table, "Carey gazed at him uneasily; she was thinking of Miss Price. Would he, she began to wonder, give quite the right impression?" (*Bed-Knob,* 139). After Emelius has returned to the past, she draws on her sense of fair play to engineer another meeting between the two lovers: "You remember we asked you whether if we promised not to stay a minute, a second, when we took him back, you would let us go later and visit him properly" (*Bed-Knob,* 158).

Carey's reactions during and after the rescue of Emelius indicate the growth of her character. Whereas during the duel between Miss Price and the witch doctor, Carey breathed the woman's name like a fan at a football match, now she breathes her name, urging Miss Price to save a life: "Miss Price . . . Miss Price. . . . Save him. Oh please, save poor Emelius" (*Bed-Knob,* 172). The girl who had at first embraced the injured Miss Price because it was the thing to do now sobs with joy because her friend is still alive. In *The Magic Bed-Knob,* Carey had replied to Miss Price's explanation of the fairness of using magic for the flower show with "I see" (*Bed-Knob,* 60). When Carey is informed that money from the sale of the house will be given to charity, "[t]o compensate this century for the loss of an able-bodied woman" (*Bed-Knob,* 184), Carey again says, "I see" (*Bed-Knob,* 184). She intuitively perceives that the match she has been desiring and quietly but deliberately promoting has been made. Her desire for the adult happiness of the woman she has grown to love has been achieved.

It is fitting that the closing focus of the novel is on Carey. She has matured the most of the three children. Wandering dreamily away from Charles and Paul as they visit the ruins of Emelius's house, she reports to them her fantasy of the lovers arriving at and entering their home. The almost young lady that she has become, Carey imagines adult love in a manner appropriate for someone her age. The closest of the children to Miss Price, she is the only one who can hear her friend's final words.

Charles plays a critical role in the adventures of the story. The shy, retiring boy of the first book becomes a leader of the children. He has taken up boxing lessons at school; he raises the subject of the bed-knob after Carey reads Miss Price's advertisement; and he knows where to find it. He is the most disappointed at Miss Price's rejection of magic, as he had most wanted the adventures; however, when there is a possibility of another magic trip, he takes an active role in trying to persuade Miss Price, skillfully praising her: "you were wonderful—professionally speaking" (*Bed-Knob,* 122). When the children enter Emelius's lodging, Charles does something he has never done before: he steps forward on his own initiative to speak to an adult, inquiring about what century they have entered. The extent of his development is apparent during the rescue scene. He announces to Carey that they should leave the old barn, in which they are hiding, to find Emelius. While Carey cries after the crash of Miss Price's broomstick, Charles slips away, seizes Miss Price's sword, and frees Emelius. He removes the man's overcoat, the better to disguise him; takes him from the stake; sharply tells Carey to be quiet; says that there is nothing to be done for the apparently dead Miss Price, noting that she would expect them to be sensible; and leads them on his painfully burned feet back to the bed. Charles has become a quiet hero.

Of course, the greatest change takes place in Miss Price. The lonely spinster and secret witch, who had spent a life of giving—care for the sick and piano lessons to children—and who had wanted to fulfill her gift of witchcraft, gives her heart to Emelius and performs her greatest magic during the rescue scene. The shy, reserved woman who dislikes strangers becomes an even greater friend to the children and falls in love with an unknown man from the past.

When the children's mother meets her, Miss Price displays those lady-like aspects of her character that the Bedfordshire villagers have come to equate with her entire personality. Her gift for magic, however, which she believes she has rejected, has merely been repressed: she has bought Aunt Beatrice's bed; she hides the bed-knob; and she takes the trip with Paul to see if the spell still works. When the children demand a trip to the past, her reluctance is based on a genuine feeling of responsibility for them. Whereas in *The Magic Bed-Knob,* she had agreed to their going as a means of buying their silence, now she acquiesces because she sees the justice of their argument, thinks the trip would be educational, and is moved by Charles's flattering reference to her professional abilities.

Her emotions and reactions on their return differ from those of the first book. Then, she had been curious to discover if the spell had worked and relieved that her secret was still safe. Now, after a restless night, during which she was "caught between two sets of fairnesses. What was fair . . . to the children was hardly fair to the parents" (*Bed-Knob,* 136), and during which she worried about the dangers of time travel and was annoyed that she had not provided a weapon in case of danger, she is extremely relieved when Carey enters her room.

The arrival of Emelius brings Miss Price new complications and the opportunities for emotional growth. Although she is flustered because no man has stayed in her house since her father died and she does not remember men's habits and attitudes, she nevertheless wishes to make a good impression, wearing her best pink blouse. Her love of neatness is at war with the pleasure she takes in Emelius's flattery. She is upset by his lack of table manners and will allow him to stay only on the condition that he have a bath and a haircut and send his clothes to the cleaners. She tries to hide her enjoyment of his compliments, laughing "a little deprecatingly" (*Bed-Knob,* 142) as she discusses her craft and "blushing slightly" (*Bed-Knob,* 140) at his praise. The first aspect of Emelius that impresses her is that he is a professional magician, the first she has met. Later she is amazed at his knowledge of the plants in her garden.

Emelius is the appropriate mate for Miss Price, for as Carey recognizes, they have much in common. In addition to their professional interests, they are, as Miss Price later tells Carey, "two lonely people. We shall be better together" (*Bed-Knob,* 185). Still, like the physical qualities of their laboratories, their personalities are not identical but complementary. Emelius has been a reluctant necromancer, moving from the country to work for a master who shattered his belief in magic. His adult life has been filled with a fear of being discovered and executed and with a feeling of inadequacy at never having successfully performed even the simplest spell. Miss Price, born with the gift for magic, has had to postpone her training until middle age and then has had no master, only a correspondence course; she feared that discovery would destroy her ladylike reputation, yet secretly yearned for approval of her talents. Emelius clings to her "as the one unassailable force in the midst of nightmarish havoc" (*Bed-Knob,* 151); she offers security and, as a true magician, restores his faith in the magic arts. He brings out her maternal instincts. After his bath, she clips his hair, asks to see his nails, knots his tie, and straightens his collar, all as if he were her little boy. He becomes her charge, her responsibility. Miss Price, the teacher of piano, summertime "mother" of the Wilsons, and vicarious participator in adult relationships through reading romance novels, has found in Emelius someone she can teach, mother, and, although she does not yet know it, love.

After Emelius has been returned to the seventeenth century, Miss Price gradually realizes the depth of her affection for him. At first she hides it from herself, treating the children sharply and throwing herself into household activities. Yet she is the one who brings up the subject of Emelius to the children, expressing worry about how he may have fared during the riots that followed the Great Fire. She takes charge of the rescue expedition. Speaking to the imprisoned necromancer in a calm, everyday voice, she tells him, like a fussing mother, "Tidy yourself up a bit and you'll feel better" (*Bed-Knob,* 166). The marvel of her trick of "intrasubstantiary-locomotion" is that, given her professed tendency to forget the few spells she has memorized when she becomes flustered, she successfully sends her broomstick into the middle of the crowd. Although the trick does not directly free Emelius, it scatters the crowd in terror, making it possible for Charles to release him.

After the return home, she quickly and efficiently arranges for the couple's departure to Emelius's seventeenth-century Bedfordshire cottage. Among the clutter she packs onto the bed are a silver cream jug and silver spoons. Are these objects from a hope chest she can now use? In the seventeenth-century setting, Miss Price will probably no longer use or even be able to use her magic. The dangers are too great; she has burned her books; and she has a poor memory for spells. She has the warm heart, bravery, and gentleness that she had once told the children were as good as magic.

There need be no third book to the series. Without Paul to do the wishing, the bed can no longer travel and will remain in the seventeenth century, where it will no doubt be the Joneses' wedding bed.[16] More important, Carey and Charles have grown far beyond the young, wondering children they were. Paul has shrunk to insignificance in the plot. Miss Price has found fulfillment in a loving and suitable marriage. Closure has been achieved.

A Precursor of Literary Greatness

Although a later critic referred to *The Magic Bed-Knob* and *Bonfires and Broomsticks* as "two mediocre stories,"[17] the initial enthusiasm for the books has not diminished. The combined *Bed-Knob and Broomstick,* published in 1957, no doubt to capitalize on the success of the first two Borrowers books, remains in print, and the 1971 motion picture starring Angela Lansbury as Miss Price is now available as a videocassette.

In addition to telling an exciting story and skillfully developing character and theme, Mary Norton's first two novels display writing talents that achieved their fullest expression in *The Borrowers:* humor, careful use of detail, and the ability to make magic plausible. Her description of Miss Price's workroom combines these three qualities very well. No set piece, it advances character and plot and creates atmosphere. Seen through the wondering eyes of Carey, the carefully described room contains the standard witch's supplies and paraphernalia, all of which are listed. Each glass jar has a neatly typed label; records of both successful and unsuccessful experiments are placed in file cabinets; notebooks are arranged on shelves. Moreover, Miss Price has added personal touches to the room. For example, she has painted the signs of her zodiac chart in watercolors. She is annoyed at the difficulty of ordering supplies and speaks sharply to Carey when the girl hands her the wrong notebook. In terms of plot, although the purpose of the scene has been to test the efficacy of the spell on the bed knob, the detailed description of the laboratory and Miss Price's reactions helps to establish the reality of the magic that is to follow and further reveals her character. Presented by Norton as an organized, tidy, and fussy middle-aged spinster, she does have a hidden side, one she is secretly proud of and desires to have recognized.

The entire portrayal of Miss Price is, as Marcus Crouch has noted, a masterpiece of humor: "Much of the fun of this book . . . comes from this basic incongruity. Miss Price could pass for a member of the Women's Institute . . . but she is a witch" (Crouch 1972, 107). Incongruity exists not only between Miss Price's public and private lives but also within this private life: she is a neat and fussy witch. Yet the humor of the character portrayal is tempered with what Crouch has called "tenderness and understanding" (Crouch 1972, 116). These qualities can be seen in Norton's frequent references to Miss Price's dominant facial feature, her long sharp nose. At first, it is seen as an aspect of her angular, bony appearance. When Carey embraces Miss Price before the departure to London, "she felt the wetness of a tear on Miss Price's long nose" (*Bed-Knob,* 93), and when she returns to spend the second summer, she thinks: "it was a reassuring nose; it was Miss Price" (*Bed-Knob,* 107). When the woman peers into Emelius's cell, the nose is "a pink-tipped banner of indignation and wrath" (*Bed-Knob,* 165), and when she discovers the children have disobeyed her by leaving the bed, "the tip of her nose was an angry pink" (*Bed-Knob,* 180). The use of such a nose to portray character is humorous, but the emotions revealed through the descriptions are those which make Miss Price such an admirable person. In many ways, Price's facial features are like those conventionally applied to witches and intended to imply the supposedly evil characteristics of such women. Here, however, the depiction of Miss Price's nose helps to reveal her positive qualities, some of which are made evident through the good uses to which she puts her witch's training.

The developing relationship between Miss Price and Emelius Jones is also portrayed with humor and compassion. The first meeting between the two is a comedy of manners, as Miss Price is flustered, annoyed, and pleased, while he, battling weariness and confusion, is effusive in his flattery and filled with awe and admiration at meeting a successful witch.

Socially inept but interested in each other, the two lonely people are constantly prompted by Charles and Carey who, although children, are much more experienced at breakfast-table conversation.

In her first two books, Mary Norton writes under the influence of various genres of children's literature and uses the techniques of fiction writing in a fairly straightforward, although very skillful, manner. Yet her treatment of plot, theme, and character anticipates abilities that will achieve their fullest expression in her next and greatest novel, *The Borrowers*. The precise use of detail to make the implausible or impossible convincing is the bedrock on which the success of *The Borrowers* rests. The ironic reversals of expectations—visiting an uninhabited island and finding cannibals, anticipating magic at Miss Price's to discover that she has given it up—are a plot staple of the Borrowers series. The gradual revelation of Miss Price's history and character as the children get to know her better parallels the reader's and Arrietty's unfolding awareness of the various adults the Clocks meet on their adventures. Charles's change from timid, shy boy to heroic rescuer of Emelius prefigures the heroic growth of the boy in *The Borrowers*. Finally, the relationship between the Wilson children and Miss Price is an anticipation of the relationships between Kate and Miss May, Arrietty and Miss Menzies, and James and Mildred.

Chapter Three

Greatness Achieved

The Borrowers

In 1972, 20 years after its publication, British critic Nigel Hand wrote of *The Borrowers* that it "challenges comparison with the most successful work in the field."[1] His opinion echoed the judgment of Marcus Crouch, who believed that "of all the winners of the Carnegie Medal, it is the one book of unquestioned, timeless genius."[2] The novel was an instant success, winning the (British) Library Association's Carnegie Medal as the best children's book of the year. Enthusiastic reviewers praised the exciting plot, skillful characterization, precise use of details, convincing quality of the highly improbable events, and above all, both the originality of the author's conception and her superb mastery of language in presenting it.

As Hand noted, however, "Only those writers who are possessed by, and in possession of, a serious theme, can stir delight to the point where feelings are not merely activated, but awakened, refreshed, and truly re-created" (Hand, 38). Not surprisingly, critics studying what psychologists Margaret and Michael Rustin call "deep structures"[3] have searched for the elements they believe give *The Borrowers* the resonance that has contributed to its staying power. The patterns of the female bildungsroman; the themes of social tension in the modern world, the power of creative imagination, and the relationship between sight and insight; the relevance of the frame story—all have been examined as highly significant elements of meaning.

Clearly, the meaning and importance of *The Borrowers* does not depend on just one or even a few of the elements critics and reviewers have noted. It is not just a matter of a well-told, exciting story with believable characters; nor is it just the fact that these are informed by deeper structures. The novel is greater than the sum of its techniques, contents, and themes. Like the bed quilt made by Mrs. May and Kate at the end of *The Borrowers,* it is a new creation, woven from old materials and by a variety of techniques into a seamless unity. To understand this creation, it is helpful to examine the materials and techniques, first individually and later together, as they form the unified creation, *The Borrowers*. The novel examines how individuals, most specifically Arrietty, grow and mature through their increased understanding of themselves in relation to their families, their natural environments, and their pasts, and how they create stories of their lives as part of this process of understanding and growth.

The Plot: Being Seen and Its Results

The highly original concept that is the basis of the plot provides, once again, an example of tradition and individual talent. Stories of little people or fairies are an essential part of British folklore, and since the time of Jonathan Swift's *Gulliver's Travels* (1726), many fictions have been written about tiny people in contact with human beings. Drawing on these traditions, Norton postulates the existence of a race of six-inch-tall people, who differ from human beings mainly in size and who live beneath the floorboards or in the walls of old country homes. They subsist by borrowing from human beings—that is, by taking objects, materials, bits of food, and even names, which they ingeniously adapt to their own needs. Like the events in *pourquoi,* or explanatory folktales, their activities offer possible explanations for the frequent, mysterious disappearance of small objects. Life is precarious for them: not only are they in danger of being seen by human beings, but once they are seen, Borrower traditions dictate emigration to ensure survival. *The Borrowers* is the story of one family of these tiny people, the Clocks—Pod, Homily, and their daughter, Arrietty, the last remaining Borrowers in a large house that used to contain many Borrowers and human beings. Their story is told by an old woman, Mrs. May, who recounts their adventures to her niece, Kate. Although the woman has never seen a Borrower, she learned about them from her brother, who, many years ago, as a young invalid recuperating in the old home, met and interacted with the Clocks.

Although the plot seems to unfold effortlessly, daily and special events flowing one into the other, it is carefully constructed around the idea of being seen and the consequences thereof for Borrowers and human beings. The narrative begins on a spring day. Arrietty, restless and disgruntled, writes in her diary, and Homily, snappish and worried, prepares dinner as they wait for Pod to come home from a borrowing expedition. When he returns, Arrietty is sent to bed so that he can tell Homily that he has just been seen by a boy and that the family must immediately emigrate. Later, when they explain to Arrietty the facts of life—the dangers and consequences of being seen by human beings—and the fact that Pod has been seen, they are surprised when the girl expresses hope that the family may emigrate and anger at being cooped up. They agree to allow her to accompany her father on a borrowing trip.

On the momentous day, after Pod has given Arrietty permission to explore outdoors, she is discovered by the boy who had seen her father. In the ensuing conversation, both are amazed to learn about the existence of large numbers of members of the other's species, talk about their lives, and depart with an agreement that Arrietty will teach the boy to read in return for his delivering a letter to the Hendrearys, Borrower relatives who had emigrated to a distant field.

One evening, after her father has gone to visit Great-Aunt Sophy, the sherry-drinking, invalid owner of the house, Arrietty sneaks to the boy's bedroom, where she learns that he has brought a letter from the Hendrearys. Discovered by her father, she is taken home, where she tells about her first meeting with the boy. Pod is angry at the danger in which she has placed them; Homily, distraught at the renewed possibility of emigration; and Arrietty, adamant about the necessity of communicating with their relatives in order to save the race. Later that night, the boy brings furniture from the doll's house for their home. His action begins "a golden age" (*Borrowers,* 130) of borrowing. Homily is delighted, although disappointed that no one can see their new wealth; Pod is exhausted from the constant rearranging of the furniture; and Arrietty is overjoyed that she, in exchange for the treasures, is allowed to read every day to the boy, enjoying his friendship, the knowledge both are acquiring from the books he brings, and the opportunity of spending time outdoors.

Mrs. Driver, the housekeeper, misses objects the boy takes from the drawing room, however, and sets out to catch the thief. Wrenching up the kitchen floorboards, she finds to her horror not only the missing objects but also three tiny people, scurrying for hiding places. Although Crampfurl, the gardener, scoffs at her account of seeing hundreds of little creatures, he agrees that it is a matter for the police. When she discovers the boy in the kitchen attempting to rescue the Clocks, she locks him in his bedroom.

At this point, the direct narration of the plot ceases, for as Mrs. May tells Kate, her brother never saw the Borrowers again. When the girl protests that it is not fair to stop telling the story at this point, Miss May then recounts later events: the boy's continued imprisonment, Mrs. Driver's elaborate preparation for the extermination of the creatures, and her forcing him to watch the operation as he awaits the arrival of a taxi to take him on the first stage of his journey back to India. At the last moment, the boy acts heroically. Seizing a pickax left unattended by one of the exterminators, he rushes into the hall, where he attempts unsuccessfully to batter open the newly sealed hole behind the clock that had been the Borrowers' only exit from their home, and then outside where he pries loose the grating near the Clocks' kitchen. Not knowing whether his efforts have been successful, he enters the taxi. As Mrs. May assures Kate, however, his efforts were successful. A year later, she had visited the house and left a sack of food and doll's house furniture in a field near a badger set to which she thought the tiny family might have gone. The sack was not there the next day; but instead she found a tiny acorn teacup and smelled hot pot. In the novel's last chapter, she and Kate imaginatively hypothesize how the Clock family might have set up its new home.

The plot of *The Borrowers* is both intriguing and exciting. The reader delights in seeing a miniature life-style, amazing because of its tiny scale and its similarity to human life-styles, and vicariously participates in the day-to-day danger of the Clocks' lives and the extreme danger that results from their having been seen. One of the ways Norton creates a convincing story and enables readers to achieve willing suspension of disbelief is through precise, detailed description of the setting, thus allowing them to visualize the unfamiliar locales of many of the actions and to appreciate the characters who live there. One critic has jokingly hypothesized the idea of the author "crawling around on her hands and knees, attempting to see the world from a Borrower's point of view."[4] Norton's first requirement was, as this critic implies, to depict the physical details of setting from the perspective of the Borrowers, so that the reader could better understand and sympathize with the ingenuity and courage of these characters whose lives depend on their ability to live in constant proximity to and in constant dependence on and danger from human beings. She achieves this in part by showing how human objects that are commonplace and small are given surprising uses, being transformed into Borrower-size equivalents of larger objects familiar to human beings. For example, in the passageways leading from their home to the entrance beneath the clock, Pod has placed numerous obstacles, using "all kinds of things for these gates—a flat leaf of a folding cheese grater, the hinged lid of a small cash-box, squares of pierced zinc from an old meat-safe, a wire fly swatter" (*Borrowers*, 13). How small these beings must be if such items can serve as gates; how courageous to venture into human domains to find and fetch them; and how clever to devise these functions for them. The same use of details is seen in the description of the family sitting room: sheets of discarded letters serve as wallpaper, postage stamps as pictures, stacked matchboxes as chests of drawers. The only item that is tiny by human standards, a set of miniature Victorian volumes, is as large to Arrietty as a church Bible would be to readers. Indeed, Tom Thumb, the two-foot midget after whom the books were named, "would seem a giant to a Borrower" (*Borrowers,* 19).

If within the home of the Clocks small human objects are made normal-size for Borrowers, when they enter the human world, the reverse is true. What is normal or small for human beings becomes huge for the Borrowers. The dark interior of the grandfather clock has "cave-like shadows" (*Borrowers,* 60); "the edges of the rugs [are] like richly colored islands in a molten sea" (*Borrowers,* 61); the doormat "rose knee deep before [Pod] like a field of chestnut corn" (*Borrowers,* 62); the steps are "terraced cliffs" (*Borrowers,* 62). While the scale of objects in the front hall is formidable to a Borrower, that of other objects is terrifying. The stove from beneath which Pod must sometimes emerge to borrow was at one time "a glowing inferno, dropping white-hot coals" (*Borrowers,* 56). Beyond the house, the world of nature is equally large. Petals are "curved, like shells" (*Borrowers,* 68); a clump of wood violets and clover is "a jungle" (*Borrowers,* 69); a primrose can be "held . . . like a parasol" (*Borrowers,* 69); and beads of dew roll "like marbles" (*Borrowers,* 69). In her descriptions of objects in the house, Norton defamiliarizes the familiar, not only creating a highly imaginative setting but also emphasizing the courage and cleverness of the Clock family, who are able to adapt to and survive in a world that may seem mundane to readers but is of epic proportions and sometimes danger to the Borrowers.

Not only are the physical details precisely described, but also they are carefully arranged. Norton may well have used the understanding of set design and stage lighting acquired in her years in the theater to display settings in a way that brought their importance to the attention of readers. In a play, the main focus of the action would be the Clocks' subfloor apartment. The sitting room, kitchen, and bedrooms would occupy the stage, with lights falling and rising to emphasize where events were occurring. The dimness beyond would suggest the lengths of tunnels that lay between the rooms and the entrance; to one side would be the grating out of which Arrietty often looked. The attentive reader, like an audience in a theater, can see not only the details of the setting but the overall arrangement of the Clocks' world.

The setting is not just concretely visualized and precisely laid out; it is also presented symbolically, as the opening sentence of the direct narration, which may be an echo of J. R. R. Tolkien's *The Hobbit*, implies: "It was Pod's hole—the keep of his fortress, the entrance to his home" (*Borrowers*, 13). The gates are like the drawbridge and portcullis of a medieval castle, protecting the embattled occupants from invaders. At the center is the home, a domestic place of comfort and security. Yet it is also a prison, for the gates, as Arrietty comes to realize, are to keep her in. Protected though it is, however, this home proves vulnerable: the floorboards are easily removed, allowing human beings to see the hidden dwelling. And it is a trap, for when the clock entrance is sealed, the grating cannot be removed by the Borrowers as they attempt to flee the rat-catcher's fumes. Above their home is the human world on which they depend and the source of their greatest dangers. Outside is the garden: to Arrietty, a world of freedom for which she yearns; to Homily, a place of danger and dirt that she fears and abhors.

Exciting though the plot is, Norton's characterization of the Clocks and what they call "human beans" most engages readers. Certainly, interest in characters is one reason Kate reacts so angrily when Mrs. May appears to have stopped telling the story at the point of Mrs. Driver's discovery of the Clocks and imprisonment of the boy. The creation of sequels was made possible because of Kate's and readers' need or desire to find out more about the characters in whose lives they had become so involved. Not surprisingly for a children's novel, the focus of interest is on Arrietty—a child, the first Borrower presented in the direct narration and the one whose inner thoughts are most frequently and fully delineated. As critic Lois Kuznets has noted, the novel is in large part a bildungsroman, "the rite of passage of a young girl" (Kuznets, 198). Although Kuznets questions "whether or not these books could stand up under feminist scrutiny" (Kuznets 1985a, 202), it is possible to argue that they do, that Norton, writing nearly two decades before the rapid growth of feminist consciousness and scholarship, accurately presents the pressures and conflicts experienced by a 13-year-old girl on the verge of young womanhood. This examination of Arrietty's development can best be considered in relation to the Borrower and human adults in her life.

Parents and Olympians: Adult Borrowers and Human Beings

Arrietty lives within a benevolent patriarchy ruled by Pod. He controls entrance into and exit from the home, "his fortress" (*Borrowers*, 13), by a number of complicated hairpin and safety pin locks only he knows how to open. He is a good provider, the only one who ventures out to gather furnishings and food for "his wife and child [who] led more sheltered lives . . . , far removed from the risks and dangers of the dreaded house above" (*Borrowers,* 14). Toward his wife he is indulgent, reluctantly giving in to her whims for different objects and aware of her moods, although never appearing to understand the reasons for them. Toward his daughter, he is protective, designing the gates to keep her from the dangers beyond.

Despite his kindness and abilities as a provider, Pod has considerable limitations: his pride in his own abilities and his conservatism. An ingenious craftsman and a skilled borrower—Homily tells Arrietty that he is "the best borrower that's been known in these parts since . . . before your grandad's time" (*Borrowers,* 38)—on his first borrowing trip with Arrietty, he demonstrates his skill in order to maintain his superiority over his wife and daughter. Opening the lock on one of the gates, he proudly states that neither she nor Homily could do it. When, as they pull tufts from the doormat, Arrietty complains that these hurt her tender hands, he replies that his are hardened. Benevolent and efficient though he may be, he must be in control, superior to the women for whom he ventures from home to provide.

Pod is an arch-conservative. Explaining to Arrietty the time-tested techniques of increasing the profits and decreasing the dangers of borrowing is understandable. Yet he rigidly hides behind received conventions if faced with new situations. When Homily suggests taking his daughter with him, he retorts, "I never heard of no girl going before" (*Borrowers,* 51), and he tells Arrietty, "There's rules, my lass, and you got to learn" (*Borrowers,* 64). Later he accuses her of not respecting tradition. Because of his dependence on tradition, he finds it exceedingly difficult to cope with new and surprising circumstances. He fails to take important actions at key points—not warning Arrietty of the existence of the boy, for example—and he frequently puts off making decisions. After discovering her with the boy, he tells Homily that they can do nothing that night except have supper and go to bed. In his refusal to share responsibilities, to act decisively, or to adapt quickly, he is partly responsible for the events that lead to the final catastrophe.

His most serious limitation is his protectiveness of Arrietty, although he justifies it to her on the grounds that "you're all we've got" (*Borrowers,* 46). He seems unconsciously unwilling to accept that she is growing up. This attitude would explain why he does not tell her of the boy's existence and is horrified when he sees the two talking together. He remarks about the unpredictability of the boys, yet he may also fear letting her meet a member of the opposite sex who could introduce her to a world that would free her from his conservative, paternalistic care and control. "[W]here does freedom take you?" (*Borrowers*, 50), he asks early in the novel. His literal warning to Arrietty about her candle, "Careful of the light!" (*Borrowers*, 28), may symbolize his wariness of new ideas. He had been a daring Borrower in his youth, but now considers that behavior foolish.

These observations are not meant to suggest that Pod is a negative character. He is not; however, his patriarchal authority is one factor with which Arrietty must contend if she is to mature. Ironically, he inadvertently and unknowingly makes it possible for her to make her first steps toward freedom. His belief that he is the best one to gather brush from the doormat gives her the time to wander into the garden, where she sees the boy. Later, in order to impress her with his ability, he shows her the techniques of climbing with a hat pin, thus giving her knowledge she will use to climb the stairs to visit the boy in his bedroom.

In contrast to Pod, Homily is someone from whom Arrietty can learn, both directly and by example, and someone who plays a major role in fostering the girl's maturing process. Critics and reviewers have termed Homily fussy, distracted, emotional, house-proud, and snobbish. To these can be added the adjectives *self-centered* and *manipulative*. She is all these by turns and often several simultaneously. In some ways, she is an unpleasant, unsympathetic character. Although she had mocked Aunt Lupy's affected manners and pretensions, when her own house is grandly refurnished with the boy's borrowings, she too becomes affected and snobbish, pronouncing *parquet* exactly as her sister-in-law had, asking Pod to build a drawing room, and regretting that there are no other people to whom she can display her possessions. Her horror of the prospect of emigration is caused as much from the thought of being with her sister-in-law and in dirty, uncivilized conditions, as from perceptions of real or imagined dangers. She is not above nagging Pod into acquiescence to her desires, and her worry over his late return home is self-indulgent guilt as much as concern for his safety. Nonetheless, Homily has many positive virtues, not the least of which are her devotion to and concern for her family. She is proud of Pod's unquestioned skill and reputation as a Borrower and of Arrietty's ability as a reader. She is genuinely relieved at Pod's return from his expeditions and is curious to hear about Arrietty's first trip beyond the gates of their apartment. She works hard and willingly at creating a home for them.

In studying Homily's character, the important question is not, What is it? but, How has it become that way? Answers can help to explain the significant role she plays in Arrietty's maturation. Since the early years of her marriage and certainly since the emigration of the Hendrearys, Homily has lived within the confines of the floorboard apartments, her only company her child and her husband. She is totally dependent on Pod for all the materials needed for homemaking, and her main contribution to his activities has been her suggestion that he use a pin and tape device for easier climbing. If she is house-proud, it is because, being house-bound, she depends on her home for a basic sense of self-worth and accomplishment. Her manipulations are sometimes the only way she can get the materials for the homemaking activities so important to her.

Yet Homily's life has not always been so lonely and restricted. In *Poor Stainless,* a story published in 1971, Homily reminisces about her childhood. Working at a routine task with her daughter, she recounts an event in which a very young Borrower went missing for a week and all the other Borrowers, male and female, young and old, spent a day searching through the house. "Somehow," Homily remarks to Arrietty, "I don't seem to forget that morning, though nothing much happened really" (*Poor,* 23). The most memorable aspect of Homily's story is not the account of the search but her description of her responses to the new world she experienced. She speaks of her breathless amazement at seeing the bright morning room and the elegant Overmantel who lived in it. She recalls that, when she had followed her uncle out of the room: "he turns away, and I go after him crying a little—I wouldn't know for why" (*Poor,* 22). She had been profoundly moved by the space, light, and beauty and saddened at leaving it. This, however, was not her only trip upstairs. Almost inadvertently, she lets slip to Arrietty the fact that, after an initial trip to the scullery for the search party organization, she would sneak back there. "I liked the scullery," she tells the girl, ". . . with the sunshine coming through the yard door and falling down on that old brick floor" (*Poor,* 16). Years later, the strongest emotions evoked by her memory of the events are anger and indignation that Stainless had enjoyed a week in the outside world: "'He'd enjoyed every minute of it!'" Homily's voice rose. "'He'd had one wild, wicked, wonderful, never-to-be-forgotten week of absolute, glorious freedom.' . . The chiffon between Homily's fingers seemed to dance with indignation. . . . '[W]e never did think it was fair!' Crossly, she shook out the chiffon" (*Poor,* 31–32). Homily had once had a taste of the world beyond the confines of her home, had understood the nature of freedom, but had never had a chance to fulfill her yearning for it. To paraphrase William Wordsworth, shades of the prison house had closed upon the growing girl. Nigel Hand has postulated that "Through the character of Homily Mary Norton registers some of the tensions of life in a mobile and technological society, with all its uncertainties and loss of traditional bearings; and with great economy she shows what unproductive strategies it can generate" (Hand, 54). Even so, the negative elements of Homily's character, particularly the anxiety Hand emphasizes, are probably not so much a result of sociological circumstances as they are a repression in Homily's adult life of the desire for freedom that had been awakened in her as a girl.

Despite her repressed life and perhaps because of it, Homily does play an important role in enabling Arrietty to leave the confines of their home. She opposes the procrastinating Pod, saying they are going to tell Arrietty about his having been seen, and dominates—with many humorous digressions in which she judges other snobbish Borrowers—the ensuing conversation. It is her decision that Pod take the girl on a borrowing trip and her insistence that lead to Arrietty's making the first excursion. "Why not?" she tells her objecting husband. "Let her just see at any rate" (*Borrowers*, 57). Her choice of a specific day to ask Pod to get the bristles from the front doormat and to take Arrietty with him seems to have been carefully thought out, for she later tells her daughter, who speaks to her from outside the grating, that the door is always open on the first day of spring. Homily's knowledge of the open door was perhaps gained during the secret excursions of her youth; whether this is the case or not, she has made it possible for Arrietty to pass through an open door, across a threshold. Although she explains that training Arrietty as a Borrower would be valuable in the event of an injury to Pod and in their old age, she may well recognize in her daughter her own youthful excitement in the now thwarted need for freedom. To repress it in Arrietty would be to doom her daughter to a life such as her own has become. Without Homily's initial assistance, the freedom Arrietty eventually achieves would probably not have been possible.

Unlike the last two adult Borrowers in the big house, who live in a loving relationship with each other, the last of the three human beings—Great-Aunt Sophy, Mrs. Driver, and Crampfurl—coexist in a state that borders on hostility. Mrs. Driver sees Great-Aunt Sophy only to deliver her nightly decanter of Fine Old Pale Madeira and Crampfurl only to share with him a stolen bottle of the port. Unlike Pod and Homily, whose protection of Arrietty is benevolently motivated, the human beings, as was Aunt Beatrice in *The Magic Bed-Knob,* are like Kenneth Grahame's Olympians in their relationship with the boy, viewing him as at best an intrusion into their lives. Their actions are in contrast to the kindliness of old Mrs. May to Kate and the nurturing of Homily to Arrietty, respectively. Crampfurl has virtually nothing to do with the boy. In fact, Crampfurl seems to be in the story basically as someone to whom Mrs. Driver can complain and as someone who can question the veracity of her sighting of the Borrowers. The focus is on Great-Aunt Sophy and, to a much greater degree, Mrs. Driver.

Since a hunting accident 20 years earlier, Sophy has withdrawn from an active life, and her children have died or left home. Homily sympathetically recognizes her loneliness, remarking about her drinking, "She had so few pleasures, poor soul" (*Borrowers,* 81). Her only friendship is with Pod, whom she believes a product of her inebriation. Even the one visit by Homily was important to her: "She perked up like anything," Arrietty tells the boy, "and kept asking for her" (*Borrowers,* 81). Still, Pod is important to her only as a listener to her repeated narrations about the long-gone days of glory. Her name, Sophy, is ironic, for even though she gives the boy his lessons, she does not possess the wisdom it implies. In many ways, she is a failed crone, not providing young people with the insights into life her age ought to have given her.

Mrs. Driver, whose name symbolizes her domineering personality, has "ruled supreme" (*Borrowers,* 18) for many years. The boy's description of her and her conversations, overheard by Arrietty, reveals how much she relishes control, threatening the boy for rearranging the doormat and refusing to perform many household labors she considers beneath her. Her need to maintain her control after the discovery of the thefts from the morning room is reflected in the fact that the last page of chapter 17 and nearly all of chapter 18, the final chapter of direct narrative, focus mainly on her thoughts and actions.

A thief, not a borrower, Mrs. Driver has considered a "drop of Madeira here, a pair of old stockings there, a handkerchief or so, an odd vest, or an occasional pair of gloves . . . within her rights" (*Borrowers,* 136). Thievery by someone else is, however, another matter. Eager to maintain the security provided by her control of the house, she fears that someone is trying to trap her, perhaps even Great-Aunt Sophy. When she finds the boy in the kitchen, she imprisons him, lying to her mistress that he has a cold, making communication between them impossible. She also decides to exterminate the Borrowers, sealing their avenue of escape and engaging the ratcatcher, experiencing an evil delight in anticipation of success. "[A] malicious gleam, a look of triumph" (*Borrowers*, 154) is in her eyes when she apprehends the boy; and she envisions that the old woman will "change her tune, like enough, when I take [the Clock family] up afterwards, laid out in sizes, on a clean piece of newspaper" (*Borrowers*, 163). She forces the boy into the kitchen to watch the extermination and is eager to return from taking him to the train station, to be "in at the death!" (*Borrowers*, 172).

Nonetheless, her attempt to reestablish her mastery is thwarted. Crampfurl doubts her sighting; Ernie Runacre, the young policeman she had tried to control years before, smirks at her; and Great-Aunt Sophy believes she has been drinking. The old woman seems to have known all along about her theft of the Madeira. Although readers are not told what happened on her return from the train station, they can well imagine how Mrs. Driver must have felt when informed that no little people had been found. No one would believe that she actually saw what she reported. She has not been able to capture these tiny people and has been thwarted by a boy. Mrs. Driver is as vulnerable in her world as the Borrowers are in theirs.

The Brave New Worlds of Arrietty and the Boy

Arrietty and the boy grow toward maturity partly in opposition to these repressed parents and Olympians. That their relationship to each other shows growth is appropriate, for while each is a lonely, isolated child, each complements the other, much as do Miss Price and Emelius Jones in *Bed-Knob and Broomstick* and James and Dulcibel in *Are All the Giants Dead?* In part because they differ in size and gender, but more important in relationship to the adults in their lives, in the source of their knowledge of the world at large, and in their temperaments, they are able to help each other. The unique qualities each possesses are beneficial to the other.

Arrietty is constrained not only by the gates and gratings of her apartment, the paternalism of her father, and the fussy restrictions of her mother but also by the limits of her knowledge of the world. She can see only a small patch of land and sky from her grating, and the relevant book in her library, *Tom Thumb's Gazetteer of the World*, is probably small in content as well as in size. Similarly, her knowledge of the past is limited. From Homily, she has received a gossipy and somewhat biased account of the many Borrower families who once lived in the great house and reports of interesting incidents that occurred before her birth; from her father, the time-honored conventions and ethics of borrowing. In her diary and proverb book are only brief sentences noting significant historical events for each day of the year.

To Arrietty, the most interesting person in the family mythology is Eggletina, Uncle Hendreary's daughter, who at age 13, the same age as Arrietty, had wandered outside, never to be seen again. Before Pod and Homily tell Arrietty of Eggletina's presumed fate, being eaten by the cat, Arrietty has compared herself with her cousin, wishing that she too could have had a mouse for a pet. When she finds out what happened, Arrietty continues the comparison, telling her parents, "I bet she just ran away because she hated being cooped up. . . . Like I do" (*Borrowers,* 49). It is ironic that the only peer example in her life is an apparently long-dead cousin she has never seen.

The direct narrative begins with the focus on Arrietty. Although the girl likes the coziness of her home, she is angry at her mother's asking for help with chores, kicking "ill-temperedly" (*Borrowers,* 14) at a potato and speaking rudely to Homily, whom she horrifies by announcing, "I could climb a curtain. . . . I could borrow" (*Borrowers,* 25). At the edge of womanhood, she is restless and near rebellion. Confined physically and psychologically, she yearns for the freedom of the outside world represented to her by the limited view seen through the grating.

Her repressed desires are partly released when, after Pod's return, her parents tell her about his having been seen and Eggletina's fate and then announce that she will soon be allowed to accompany her father borrowing. Before the conversation, she had been in her bedroom "[staring at] without seeing" (*Borrowers,* 35) the cigar-box roof depicting "lovely painted ladies dressed in swirls of chiffon [and blowing] long trumpets against a background of blue sky" (*Borrowers,* 35). Returning to her bedroom later, she "gazed up at her painted ceiling" (*Borrowers,* 52), on which "the lovely gauzy ladies blew their trumpets, silently, triumphantly, on soundless notes of glee" (*Borrowers,* 54). By noting that Arrietty is now reacting to the ceiling and by adding the words *triumphantly* and *glee,* Norton draws attention to the change in the girl's attitude as a result of the meeting. Arrietty feels as free as the floating women seem to be. After Pod and Homily tell her the facts of Borrower life, her reactions are not what they expect. On hearing of Eggletina's adventure, Arrietty only wants to know how she got out. Learning that her father has been seen, she asks if they could emigrate. She begins to cry and angrily tells her parents, "I don't think it's so clever to live on alone, forever and ever, in a great, big, half-empty house; under the floor with no one to talk to, no one to play with, nothing to see but dust and passages, no light but candlelight and fire-light and what comes through the cracks" (*Borrowers*, 49). Her mood changes when the possibility of her borrowing is raised: "'Oh—' she began in an ecstatic voice" (*Borrowers*, 51).

Norton's depiction of Arrietty's actions, perceptions, and emotions during the girl's first trip beyond the floorboard apartments gives the specific episode highly symbolic dimensions. As a learning experience, the passage through the tunnels, out from under the clock, and through the door are described as a movement from dark to light. Initially, "Arrietty saw a faint light at the end of the passage" (*Borrowers*, 60). Her first impressions of the world beyond the clock are of an almost over-whelming, "sudden blinding glimpse of molten gold" (*Borrowers*, 60). When her vision focuses, "she saw, in a glory of sunlight—like a dreamed-of gateway to fairyland—the open front door" (*Borrowers*, 61). Having passed through the literal gates constructed by Pod, gates that have imprisoned her in a darkness both physical and nonphysical, she prepares to pass through metaphorical gates that liberate her into a world of imaginative fulfillment and freedom. Significantly, moments after looking at the door, she notices her father: "Arrietty saw him scurry across the sunlit floor. Swiftly he ran—as a mouse runs or a blown dry leaf—and suddenly she saw him as 'small'" (*Borrowers*, 61). Her newly acquired perspective diminishes her father's importance; she is taking her first steps away from what feminist critic Annis Pratt has called "enclosure in the patriarchy."[5]

Venturing into the garden, Arrietty enters what Pratt calls "the green world," where Nature "becomes an ally of the woman hero, keeping her in touch with her selfhood" (Pratt 1981, 21). She walks out onto the front step and around to the side of the house, where she talks to her mother through the grate. Then she wanders away from her father, exploring among flowers, plants, insects, and birds, all of which are described by Norton in terms that make them seem huge but non-threatening to the girl. The symbolic significance of these events is apparent when we consider the verbal clichés that can be used to describe the actions. She has crossed a threshold, turned a corner (despite her father's initial prohibition against doing so), stood on the outside looking in, and wandered out of sight (and possibly out of mind) of her father. Her sense of liberation is reflected in her movements: "The stones in the path were firmly bedded and her light, soft shoes hardly seemed to touch them. How glorious it was to run" (*Borrowers*, 66). As she talks to her mother, "her toes danced on the green moss" (*Borrowers*, 66).

Appropriately, Arrietty at first sees just the boy's eye and only later hears his voice. Having moved beyond Pod's protective eye and admonishing voice, she will meet someone who, after being initially threatening, is curious and questioning. Arrietty tries to comprehend her situation by reference to the only element of family tradition that has relevance to her, thinking that what happened to Eggletina will now happen to her. But she calms herself and bravely confronts the boy, staring at his eye. Her bluff works, and she adroitly encourages his questions about reading. She is shocked when he calls her a fairy, denying that such creatures exist. Her reaction is important, for the boy, in calling her a fairy, is denying her identity as a Borrower. She knows what she is and is not as a species; she does not, as yet, know who she is as an individual. Recounting her father's exploits with pride, delineating the family mythology, and outlining the ethics of Borrowers, she defines herself only in relation to her family and tradition.

She is also ethnocentric. She calls the boy silly when he tells her there are far more people than Borrowers. Given the scale of her family's physical needs, she cannot comprehend enough material or food to supply more than a few human beings. "Human beings are for Borrowers—like bread's for butter" (*Borrowers*, 84), she announces. When the boy asks where the other Borrowers are and suggests that the Clocks are the last three, her smugness is shattered. She announces that she has decided not to read to him and begins to cry. Now it is Arrietty, not the boy, who stares "with frightened eyes" (*Borrowers*, 86), and she feels cold in the shadow he casts. The joyous optimism with which she has greeted the spring sunshine has been obscured. Kuznets has compared this scene to the biblical Fall in the Garden of Eden, a loss of innocence accompanied by an awareness of the complexity of life (Kuznets 1985a, 200). Whether or not the experience is perceived in quite these biblical terms, Arrietty has had a nonsexual awakening, a permanent loss of ethnocentric innocence, one that prepares her to see what she and other people really are, instead of what she has been told they are.

Arrietty is not yet ready to face this new world bravely. She retreats, announcing that she is going home, and is almost relieved to see her father: "how round his face was, how kind, how familiar" (*Borrowers*, 88). The yearnings for the outdoors she had felt when staring out from her grating have been somewhat qualified by her experience. Still, she returns to her home and family profoundly altered. Her restlessness, which had changed from vague, undefined yearnings to a desire to have the kind of experience Eggletina had, has a specific focus: she wishes to have the boy deliver a letter to other Borrowers as a means of saving her family and, ultimately, the race. She now views the apartment differently: "How familiar the room seemed, and homely, but, suddenly, somehow strange: the firelight flickering on the wallpaper—the line which read: '. . . it would be so charming if—' If what? Arrietty always wondered. If our house were less dark, she thought, that would be charming" (*Borrowers*, 90). During spring cleaning activities, which she had always enjoyed before, Arrietty "bang[s] about impatiently" (*Borrowers*, 96), worried that she will be unable to get a letter to the boy. The opportunity comes when she accompanies Pod on a second trip, a nighttime expedition through the darkness. When she enters the morning room, domain of the legendary Overmantels, she imagines their glamorous, luxurious life-style, but because of her meeting with the boy, wonders, "Where were they now? . . . Where could such creatures go?" (*Borrowers*, 99). Earlier, reflections about Eggletina's disappearance had made Arrietty dissatisfied with her own life; now, thoughts about the disappearance of the Overmantels raise implicit concerns for the well-being of her family.

Overhearing Mrs. Driver and Crampfurl talking about the boy's removing the doormat and searching in ferret holes, Arrietty realizes the urgency of seeing him: "I must hear what happened. I must hear if [the Hendrearys are] all right. I don't want us to die out. I don't want to be the last Borrower. I don't want . . . to live forever and ever like this . . . in the dark . . . under the floor" (*Borrowers*, 105–6). When her father is out one evening, she sneaks past the open gates and up the darkened stairs: "On the upper landing she saw an open door and a great square of golden light which like a barrier lay across the passage" (*Borrowers*, 108). A much more knowledgeable and resolute Arrietty now traverses this light and crosses this threshold. This time, she sees the complete face of the boy about whom she has some knowledge. Together, they read the letter from Uncle Hendreary, and Arrietty gains new information: her relatives are alive; her family is not the last of the race. Discovered by Pod, Arrietty responds to her parents' outbursts with considerable maturity and comprehension: "'They are frightened,' Arrietty realized; 'they are not angry at all—they are very, very frightened'" (*Borrowers*, 115). But Pod and Homily, who have had little understanding about her feelings—attributing, for example, her restlessness to spring fever and her grumpiness to feeling "seedy" (*Borrowers*, 105)—do not comprehend the motives for her actions. When she announces, "I'm trying to save the race!" (*Borrowers*, 116), Pod speaks sternly of violating tradition.

Dismissed to her bedroom, where, as earlier, she stares at the ceiling while listening to her parents talk, she feels ambivalent. She sees the complexity of her new life: "She did not want to lose [home and possessions], she realized suddenly, lying there straight and still in bed, but to have all the other things as well, adventure and safety mixed—that's what she wanted. And that . . . is just what you couldn't do" (*Borrowers*, 120). As Kuznets has noted, Arrietty is coming to terms with "the ambivalence which the child feels in relinquishing the state of secure dependency for one of dangerous responsibility for her own acts" (Kuznets 1985a, 200).

During the golden age of borrowing that follows, Arrietty learns from the boy about her place in relation to the world at large: "What worlds they would explore together—strange worlds to Arrietty. She learned a lot and some of the things she learned were hard to accept. She was made to realize once and for all that this earth on which they lived turning about in space did not revolve, as she had believed, for the sake of little people" (*Borrowers*, 132). After Mrs. Driver's discovery of the family, when Arrietty's dream of emigration is achieved, she cries for happiness: "Her wet face glistened in the candlelight; it was alight and tremulous and she raised her arms a little as though about to fly, and she swayed as she balanced on her toe-tips. . . . she closed her eyes against the brightness of the vision [of emigration]" (*Borrowers*, 151).

When last seen in the novel, she is perched at the top of the bag in which the boy has placed her family, looking outward. Arrietty's journey is by no means complete. She is like the characters at the beginning of the folktale "The Story of the Three Little Pigs," whose leaving home is only the first step on the road to maturity. She has lost her selfish concerns and her ethnocentrism, bravely moving toward the dangerous, unknown, but exciting world of adulthood.

Considering his importance to the narrative—his seeing the Borrowers and his having been seen by Mrs. Driver activate the major events of the novel—the character of the boy has received little critical attention. He is one of the reasons the Clocks are able to survive and the reason their story does. The Rustins have traced his movement from immature, lonely isolation to fulfillment (Rustin and Rustin, 70–71). Mrs. May tells Kate that "he died what they call 'a hero's death'" (*Borrowers*, 6), a British army colonel serving in India. The events of the story help to explain how such a timorous boy achieved such status. What is there about him that caused him to become involved in the Borrowers' lives, and what is there about this involvement that caused him to talk about it to his sister, Mrs. May, not only during a childhood boat trip to India but later in his life? How did his experience change his life?

The boy's physical world is infinitely less circumscribed than Arrietty's. Born in India, schooled in England, he knows, as he tells Arrietty, a great deal "about railway stations and football matches and racecourses and royal processions and Albert Hall concerts" (*Borrowers,* 86). Nonetheless, he is the baby of his family, the only boy, and unlike his sisters he cannot read. Never a strong child, he has been sent to the great house to recover from rheumatic fever. His life here is much lonelier than Arrietty's; far away from his family, he is in contact only with Great-Aunt Sophy and Mrs. Driver. He says that the former "gives me dictation and teaches me to write. I only see her in the mornings when she's cross" (*Borrowers,* 81) and that the latter "gives me my bath and hurts my bruise and my sore elbow and says she'll take a slipper to me one of these days" (*Borrowers,* 81). Significantly, Arrietty first sees the boy outside on Mrs. Driver's day off. Perhaps he finds the house as much a prison as Arrietty does and is seeking an escape, however brief.

When he meets Arrietty, he is frightened, believing her to be a fairy and threatening her with his ash stick, no doubt believing in that wood's magical potency. After she tells him about Borrowers, he replies, "smiling triumphantly" (*Borrowers,* 87), that he believes they are dying out and that she will eventually be the only Borrower left. Lonely and somewhat frightened, he reacts with anger and cruelty. He is not, however, a nasty boy: helping Pod was an act of kindness, and he wants to please Arrietty, volunteering to take a letter to the Hendrearys. His asking Arrietty if she can read is not so unusual as it might at first appear. He needs a peer, however tiny, who can help him to overcome the deficiency that makes him feel inferior to his sisters. Moreover, he can provide access to a source of knowledge she does not have: books. Above all, he is a little boy in need of a friend, or as the Rustins have suggested, "a living link with the sisters he so much misses" (Rustin and Rustin, 69). Away from his mother, cared for roughly by two Olympian women, he can find in Arrietty the female contact he needs. His sincerity and sense of obligation are revealed in the ensuing days by his continuing visits to the doormat in search of the letter, despite Mrs. Driver's repeated threats of punishment. He demonstrates his trustworthiness, cleverly evading Crampfurl's attempts to find out what he is doing in the field, thereby keeping the secret of the Clocks' existence. Disastrous though his raiding of the doll's house finally proves, his motivations are good. He had learned during his first meeting with Arrietty of the Borrowers' loss of their worldly wealth in a kitchen flood, and because of his affection for them and his wish to have Arrietty read to him, he brings them material possessions beyond "all dreams of borrowing" (*Borrowers,* 130). He grows in human understanding and compassion as well as in book knowledge.

The extent of his unselfish attachment to his new friends, his substitute family, is seen during the catastrophe, for he acts decisively in planning for their escape and is excited to learn about their proposed destination, the badger's set. He empathizes with Arrietty, understanding her emotions. When he is discovered by Mrs. Driver, he defends the Clocks against her accusations of thievery and announces that he too is a Borrower. He has come to identify with them and to see their lives from their point of view. The boy whose lip had trembled because he missed his mother now "cried his heart out under the blankets" (*Borrowers,* 156) when imprisoned in his room by Mrs. Driver. He weeps for his friends and their fate.

Apparently powerless, the boy nevertheless makes possible the Borrowers' escape through a series of actions that are selfless and courageous. Dragged into the kitchen to watch the exterminator at work, he notices a pickax, which he grabs and stealthily takes out into the hall. Unsuccessful in his attempts to dislodge the metal plate blocking the wall exit, he hears the workmen mention ventilation, remembers the grating, and, with the cab coming up the driveway, races outside and tears open the mesh. He displays a clarity and inventiveness of thought, and he shows great courage, for given his fear of the vindictive Mrs. Driver, thoughts of her anger and punishment would have been terrifying to him.

Although he never returned to the great house or learned what happened to Pod, Homily, and Arrietty, the boy continued to think of them. Mrs. May reports that on the boat to India, he would go "over the old ground, repeating conversations, telling me details again and again" (*Borrowers,* 8), and that when he and his sister had grown up, he continued to speak about the events. That he should remember and frequently recount the episodes of that summer is not surprising. His friendship and his actions had liberated the timid, insecure little boy. Like Arrietty's, it was the first summer of his freedom, the beginning of his journey to adulthood.

Re-creating the Past: Narrative Framework and
Point of View

Although early reviewers rightfully praised the originality of concept, plot, and characterization in *The Borrowers,* they gave only passing notice to another key element of the book's originality: its setting of the adventures of the Clock family within the framework of Mrs. May's telling the story to Kate. As recent critics suggest, an understanding of this framework is crucial to an understanding of the total meaning of the novel, a meaning that is greater than the significance of the Borrowers' story itself. The first chapter presents Mrs. May explaining the background of the events and how she learned about them; chapters 2 through 18 are her direct narrative of events between the times of the boy's first and last sightings of the Clocks; chapter 19 and 20 are set in the present, as Mrs. May tells Kate about the boy's last four days at the house and her visit there a year later, and the old woman and the girl create a hypothetical account of the Clocks' life after their escape from the house.

In creating the framework, Mary Norton is using an ancient storytelling technique, one in which a character recounts events in which he or she has been peripherally or centrally involved. In *Tellers and Listeners,* Barbara Hardy traces the tradition back to Homer's *Odyssey,* in which the hero reports his adventures to admiring audiences.[6] Other well-known works employing this technique include Milton's *Paradise Lost,* Coleridge's *The Rime of the Ancient Mariner,* Emily Brontë's *Wuthering Heights,* Conrad's *Heart of Darkness,* and William Faulkner's *Absalom, Absalom!* Modern literary theorists have termed these types of stories metafictions, defined by Inger Christensen as "fiction whose primary concern is to express the novelist's vision of experience by exploring the process of its own making."[7] Christensen goes on to say, "The metafictionist deals with . . . fundamental issues of communication by directing attention to the narrator, the narrative, and the narratee [the teller, the tale, and the listener/reader] in his work" (Christensen, 14). Such novels raise important questions. Why do authors chose specific tellers? Why do tellers choose to relate specific stories? Why do they choose the listeners they do? How do listeners react to the stories? And finally, how do the frame stories interact with the inner stories to influence the total meaning of the novels?

At the beginning of the English edition of *The Borrowers,* a paragraph omitted from the American edition implicitly raises these questions: "It was Mrs. May who first told me about them. No, not me. How could it have been me—a wild, untidy, self-willed little girl who stared with angry eyes and was said to crunch her teeth?"[8] Julia Davenport suggests answers that relate to achieving credibility for an improbable plot. Norton's techniques, she writes, "whet our appetites, and they lend the story a quality of truth and seriousness that keeps it from degenerating into whimsy," and Mrs. May, "a sensible, down-to-earth woman" (Davenport, 76), provides a bridge from Kate's everyday, normal world into the marvelous world of the Clock family. Moreover, Mrs. May has, through her brother, a connection to the events she narrates.

Although the framework undoubtedly fulfills these purposes, Norton could have used other techniques to achieve much the same results. To find more complete answers, we can approach the framework indirectly, comparing it with that of Faulkner's adult novel *Absalom, Absalom!* That work begins as 18-year-old Quentin Compson sits in the darkened parlor of Rosa Coldfield, an old spinster who talks about her relationship with one of the town's legendary figures, Thomas Sutpen. Initially puzzled by her having invited him to her home and her commencing the narrative, he soon realizes, "[i]t's because she wants it told, . . . so that people whom she will never see and whose names she will never hear and who have never heard her name nor seen her face will read it and know at last why God let us lose the War."[9] Mrs. May, like Rosa Coldfield, wants the story of the Clock family to be told, although, of course, her reasons are different.

Before an examination of these reasons, her narrative, which occupies chapter 2 to chapter 18, must be considered. The primary source of her information is her brother. But her telling is not simply a repetition of his telling. She had, we have seen, listened many times to his going over events and conversations. She, like Miss Price, who "pieced the pattern together" (*Bed-Knob*, 57) from the Wilson children's disjointed accounts of their first trip on the bed, has organized her brother's information into a coherent, chronological narrative. Some of the material of the story she could have supplied herself, including the detailed descriptions of the house, which she visited a year after her brother left. Her sensitive interpretations of the three female adults in the story, Homily, Great-Aunt Sophy, and Mrs. Driver, are no doubt a product of her mature wisdom and her experience as a woman. Her portrayal of her brother would be drawn from her understanding of him as both a boy and a man. Using these sources of information, Mrs. May is like the Borrowers she describes, creatively adapting old materials to make something new and purposeful. The story she tells is not presented from the point of view of her brother, from whom much of it comes; in fact, he does not appear in the narrative until chapter 9. She begins with her focus on Arrietty and portrays the girl as she relates first to her mother and father and then to the boy. Later Mrs. May considers Mrs. Driver's thoughts and motivations as she plans to capture the thieves. Mrs. May is telling a story about females, for whom she has empathy, to a female.

Just as Coleridge's Ancient Mariner had instinctive knowledge of the appropriate listener for his saga, so Mrs. May knows that Kate is the right audience for her narrative. Although three years younger than Arrietty, Kate is not unlike her: cross and often ill-tempered. Mrs. May is the one who brings up the subject of the Borrowers when Kate remarks about missing objects, and she entices the girl to ask her about these beings. "'Why so quiet, child?' asked Mrs. May one day, when Kate was sitting hunched and idle upon the hassock" (*Borrowers* English edition 1952, 8). Soon after, the old woman begins a story about Arrietty, who, as Homily complains, is also frequently silent and idle. The bildungsroman that follows is presented in a way appropriate to its receptive listener.

In telling the story, Mrs. May is like a crone, the wise old female keeper of lore and wisdom who, in myths, legends, and folktales was responsible for initiating young girls into adult life (Walker, *passim*). Her use of story as a vehicle of instruction is appropriate, for as feminist theologian Carol Christ has written: "Women's stories have not been told. And without stories there is no articulation of experience. Without stories a woman is lost when she comes to make the important decisions of her life. She does not learn to value her struggles, to celebrate her strengths, to comprehend her pain. Without stories she cannot understand herself. . . . If women's stories are not told, the depth of women's souls will not be known."[10] Mrs. May has given Kate a narrative framework with which to guide her own inner growth. But good teacher that she is, she does not present a complete, rigidly defined story, and she frequently casts doubt on the factuality of the events she narrates. Unlike Pod, who had inflexibly passed on to Arrietty the (to him) immutable concepts of borrowing, Mrs. May makes necessary a creative, questioning response. Kate must remake the story, understanding it in her own terms. This is one of the reasons that the old woman interrupts the narrative at the end of chapter 18. A tease, just as she had said her brother was, she is vexing Kate out of being an intense listener and into becoming an involved teller of the story.

The location of the telling and the activities in which the old woman and young girl are engaged are appropriate for Mrs. May's purposes. In a twilight atmosphere, suitable to the telling of such a tale, Mrs. May has been teaching Kate the techniques of sewing, "how to run-and-fell and plan a darn" (*Borrowers,* 3), and later how to quick-stitch. The specific techniques are significant. The technique of "running" involves gathering a number of stitches on a needle at one time, while "felling" is sewing pieces of cloth smoothly together in a manner that makes the joins appear seamless. Quilting, of course, involves the uniting of different colored squares of usually old material into a new object. Feminist critics have frequently seen this predominantly female activity as symbolic of women's lives and activities in general: the joining together of old elements to create something new and valuable.[11] Mrs. May teaches the techniques literally and symbolically. During the last two chapters, as they sew together the crocheted patches into a quilt, Mrs. May helps Kate gather together the pieces of information and the understanding she has acquired from hearing the direct narrative to create a unified, seamless narrative to conclude the Clocks' adventures.[12]

In wanting the story told, Mrs. May wishes not only to instruct Kate but also to fulfill her own inner needs. In performing her role as a crone, telling a story beneficial to Kate, she is achieving a sense of purpose and usefulness. A lonely person without immediate family, she is, as the Rustins have noted, a kind of Borrower herself, living in her old age with relatives: "Mrs. May is able through contact with a young girl to bring alive her own memories and overcome her own loneliness" (Rustin and Rustin, 66). Barbara Hardy's statement about D. H. Lawrence's *Sons and Lovers*—"The story is . . . a ritual, a serial telling solicited and encouraged with love. It is not a performance by one narrator, but a communion and a real conversation" (Hardy, 140)—can be applied to the conclusion of *The Borrowers,* as Mrs. May and Kate work as partners to complete the narration. In telling the story, Mrs. May is also keeping alive an important aspect of her past, for she was involved, however inconclusively or indirectly, in the lives of the Clocks, taking supplies into the fields for them. Moreover, during the retelling, she recaptures a sense of wonder and excitement. Her evasiveness with Kate near the end of the novel may be in part an attempt to hide feelings she is embarrassed to have the girl perceive. Mrs. May is like Marlow, the narrator of Joseph Conrad's *Heart of Darkness,* of whom Barbara Hardy has written,

"The imaginative narrator only tells what moves, bewilders, and tests him" (Hardy, 155).

When Mrs. May's conclusions are related to elements of the direct narrative and to the account of the Clocks' life after the escape as it is presented in *The Borrowers Afield,* however, they become suspect. In the second book of the series, based on information Kate acquires partly from Arrietty's diary, it is learned that the three Borrowers did not settle in the badger set or near the gaspipe, and they did not retrieve Mrs. May's parcel; it was found by the Hendrearys. Mrs. May claims to have gained much of her information from the miniature Memoranda that had formed part of Arrietty's library. But it is described early in Mrs. May's direct narration as having blank pages, and nowhere is there any reference to Arrietty's having written in it. Mrs. May suggests that her brother may have written in it and that both he and Arrietty formed their *e*'s in the same way. Yet in discussing the three days he was imprisoned by Mrs. Driver, she makes no reference to the boy's having written, and one wonders how a boy who could barely read was able to write cursive letters as well as the more practiced Arrietty could.

Why, at the conclusion of the novel, should author Mary Norton raise doubts about the credibility of Mrs. May's narration? Probably the intention is not to invalidate what the old woman has said all along. Although Mrs. May supplies her own interpretations of character, she has no doubt presented the facts accurately. There are many possible answers. First, not knowing what happened to them, she has been forced to invent, with Kate's help, a conclusion that will be emotionally satisfying and reassuring to her and that, because she seems to have played a role in it, will make her as significant to Kate as the boy wanted to be to his sisters. But she is embarrassed as well and tries to slip her unsubstantiated disclaimer past Kate as a means of letting herself off the hook. Finally, as she tells Kate, "Stories never really end. They can go on and on. It's just that sometimes, at a certain point, one stops telling them" (*Borrowers,* 158). With her account of her trip into the field and her hypothesis on the later lives of the Clocks, she has reached that certain point. In the words of the old folksong "Froggie Went a'Courtin'," "If you want to hear more, you must sing it yourself." And two years later, in *The Borrowers Afield,* Kate does just that, picking up the story with the aid of Tom Goodenough.

During the course of the novel, Kate moves from a rapt listener to an eager coteller. Just as the boy was changed by his involvement with Arrietty, she is changed by her involvement with the story. At the beginning, Kate is a receptive audience, eagerly responding to the bait with which Mrs. May teases her. "There can't be [little people]," she tells Mrs. May. "And yet . . . and yet sometimes I think there must be" (*Borrowers,* 4). "Please, go on," she urges. "Please tell me. . . . Try to remember. Right from the very beginning" (*Borrowers,* 7).

When Mrs. May announces at the beginning of chapter 19 that it is the end of the story, Kate reacts strongly. The English edition is more detailed than the American in depicting her response: "'But,' stammered Kate, 'You can't—I mean—'and she looked, quite suddenly, everything they had said she was—wild, self-willed, and all the rest of it. 'It's not fair,' she cried, 'it's cheating. It's —.' Tears sprang to her eyes; she threw her work down on the table and the darning needle after it, and she kicked the bag of wools which lay beside her on the carpet" (*Borrowers* English edition 1952, 140). Kate realizes that, in addition to a beginning and a middle, a story should have an end, with a strong sense of closure, "the sense that nothing necessary has been omitted from a work."[13] But her remarks are personal as well as aesthetic; she has become so involved with the lives of the Clock family that she needs to know the outcome of their dangerous journey. Requiring certainty, she asks Mrs. May a series of questions designed to elicit from the old woman an account of the boy's actions after he had been discovered by Mrs. Driver.

Mrs. May has been a very good storyteller, creating tremendous audience involvement. Kate has learned so much about the Borrowers' lives and characters and has internalized the story so well, that she is able, with Mrs. May, to create an emotionally satisfying closure to the story. Whereas in chapter 18 she was upset because Mrs. May appeared to be stopping the narrative before it was complete, in chapter 19 she is unhappy because of aspects of the narrative the old woman is supplying: "'But,' went on Kate in a despairing voice as she picked up the scissors, 'Homily would hate to arrive there all poor and destitute in front of Lupy'" (*Borrowers,* 173). She is responding this way because of the sensitive understanding of Homily she has acquired as a listener. Later, when Mrs. May speculates that Arrietty and Homily would not stray from Pod, Kate quickly counters, "Arrietty would" (*Borrowers,* 175). Although, as will be seen in *The Borrowers Afield,* their speculations on the family's new domestic arrangements will prove to be factually incorrect, they are appropriate, based on the two narrators' sensitive understanding of the characters of the two Clock females. A satisfying emotional closure has been achieved, in part as a result of Kate's growth of perception during her day of listening and then telling.

As has been noted, however, the frame story and the novel itself end on a note of skepticism and doubt. Readers do not know Kate's reaction to Mrs. May's remark that the *Memoranda* book, the alleged source of some of her information, could have been written by her brother, not Arrietty. Nonetheless, Mrs. May's statement draws attention to the metafictional nature of the story. It is, after all, a story largely created by a woman who many years earlier had heard a version of it from a brother who was known to be a tease and to have a vivid imagination. If Kate could doubt Mrs. May, who in turn could have doubted her brother, what are readers of the book to do? They must realize that the meaning of *The Borrowers* comes from the interrelationship of the parts of the work. They must consider the tale and the tellers. As Inger Christensen has noted, "A novelist's vision, or the message he wants to convey, is closely related to the form of his work" (Christensen, 151). As the boy revised reports of Clock history learned from Arrietty, Mrs. May has revised his story, and Kate, who, as the opening of the British edition makes clear, is the frame narrator of the book, revises Mrs. May. Readers must revise all of these storytellers to create the work for themselves. Just as the poet persona watching the guitar player in Wallace Stevens's poem "The Idea of Order at Key West" uses imagination to fulfill a "blessed rage for order,"[14] so too do readers of *The Borrowers* become the final authors of the story. Or, as William Faulkner remarked about the multiple storytellers in *Absalom, Absalom!* "I think that no one individual can look at truth. It blinds you. You look at it and you see one phase of it. Someone else looks at it and sees a slightly awry phase of it. But taken all together, the truth is in what they saw though nobody saw the truth intact. . . . It was, as you say, thirteen ways of looking at a blackbird. But the truth, I would like to think, comes out, that when the reader has read all these thirteen different ways of looking at the blackbird, the reader has his own fourteenth image of that blackbird which I would like to think is the truth."[15] The story of the Clock family has survived and evolved because of the sequence of interactions between tellers and listeners within the novel. By implicitly drawing attention to the metafictional nature of *The Borrowers,* Norton is asking that readers also engage in this type of interaction with her book in order to achieve an understanding, a comprehension that makes *The Borrowers* a unified, consistent work of art. Readers must become Borrowers themselves, taking the material of the novel to create a new work meaningful to themselves.

The Meaning of *The Borrowers:* Thematic Approaches

Several critics have read the novel as a reflection, commentary, and even symbolic representation of sociopolitical conditions in England during the first half of the twentieth century. Nigel Hand has commented on "the tensions of life in a mobile and technological society, with all its uncertainties and loss of traditional bearings" (Hand, 54). Kuznets has called the book a "diaspora in miniature" and related it generally and Mrs. Driver specifically to conditions in Germany during World War II: "*The Borrowers* depicts a family in extremity, one that will become displaced refugees. Like the Jews in Germany, the Clocks may have delayed too long" (Kuznets 1985a, 201). The Rustins have provided the most extended sociopolitical reading, stating that "*The Borrowers* series . . . represents a version of the English social landscape of the period of Norton's life" (Rustin and Rustin, 63), drawing parallels between Arrietty's reading ability and "the extension of post-war education"; the relationship between Crampfurl, Mrs. Driver, and Great-Aunt Sophy and that between "a repressive servant class . . . [and] the upper-class owner"; and the destruction of the Clock home and "the physical and social changes brought about in Britain by World War II" (Rustin and Rustin, 63).

Yet as these critics implicitly realize, to see the novel only in these terms is to limit its greatness. Novels do grow out of authors' relationships with and responses to their times, but if they are to have a continuing significance, they must do more. Norton herself called attention to the broader aspects of the novel: "it has something of the whole human dilemma—a microcosm of our world and the powers which rule us. In each generation, only youth is restless and brave enough to try to get out from 'under the floorboards.'"[16] As noted, critics have commented widely on the theme of the female bildungsroman. Hand states that "the fiction is always rooted in a search for secure and healthy conditions for life" (Hand, 40). He emphasizes the value of creative imagination in this process, judging the characters by their ability to use this faculty. The Rustins note the importance of achieving fulfillment by escaping from various forms of repressions and imprisonment both literal and symbolic (Rustin and Rustin, 66).

All of these themes are important, but do not explain why the novel achieves such a satisfying unity, one in which all aspects of style, technique, plot, characterization, and theme interrelate. One such unifying principle can be found in the concept of "seeing" and such related ideas as "insight" and "appearance." These concepts underlie the individual elements discussed so far and give the novel its central focus and meaning.

The first evidence of the importance of "seeing" is to be found in the language and style of the book. There are more than 350 uses of words relating to sight, words such as *saw, looked, seen,* and *eye.* While many of these words are used in a way one would expect in a novel in which characters are in possession of their visual faculties, the majority relate to character, plot, tone, and theme. For example, the novel begins with Kate *looking* at the floor; doubt as to the story's veracity is created by the fact that the principal narrator, Mrs. May, has never seen a Borrower; and Homily, on welcoming Pod back from an expedition, notices that he looks odd. Not all the references are as significant as those mentioned, but the total number of references, averaging nearly 10 a chapter, help to create a linguistic climate in which the importance of the visual motif is subtly, perhaps unconsciously, impressed on readers.

The linguistic texture of the book is used in characterization, for the Borrowers' colloquialisms also reflect the importance of seeing and being seen in their lives. "I don't see anything bad in that" (*Borrowers,* 24), the somewhat rebellious Arrietty remarks to her mother at one point. Speaking of fine china, Homily muses, "But it's once you've *had* a teacup, if you see what I mean" (*Borrowers,* 24). Worried about the possibility of their having to emigrate, Pod tells Arrietty, "[Y]ou're all we've got, see" (*Borrowers,* 46). Examples such as these, found throughout *The Borrowers,* reinforce the seeing motif. In these instances as in many others, the words relating to sight reflect the attempts of one character to make another understand his or her attitude. Thus the colloquialisms are about "insight" as well as "outsight."

It might be objected that there are many significant references to hearing, and there are. But these, significantly, are related to sight. The clock is the most notable—its noises and chimings relate to the routine by which members of the family live and a knowledge of which helps the Borrowers avoid being seen. After they are seen by Mrs. Driver, the clock is silent for the first time in 80 years. The noises of the human adults in the kitchen are an assurance, for when these are heard, the Borrowers are not seen. When Pod relates his first meeting with the boy, the first time he has been seen, "Homily *stared* at him in silence" (*Borrowers,* 30; italics mine). And as Arrietty lies quietly in her darkened room, she hears her parents talk about the consequences of being seen.

The book is primarily visual in style. Of course, writing fantasy as she is, the author must convince her readers primarily through description. But more important, the way settings are described relates to tone and meaning. The opening and closing pages of the frame narration are set in a twilight breakfast room, pervaded by a "strange silvery light" (*Borrowers,* 3) that creates an appropriate setting for the sympathetic, imaginative re-creation of the past. The principal setting, the Clocks' floorboard home, is always dimly lit, for safety requires its location deep within the house, where the family cannot be seen. Yet it embodies not only the logistics of family life but also character, for living by routine, tradition, and fear, the elder Clocks are, in a sense, benighted. The light, in this case the great outdoors, frightens them, not just because it increases the danger of being seen but because it represents a violent disruption of the dim, womblike security of their accustomed way of life. But for Arrietty, who has gazed longingly at the outdoors through her grating, the dimness of the apartment parallels the weight pressing on her yearning, restless, and youthful soul. Appropriately, the most visually vivid sections of the book are those which describe Arrietty's first venture out from under the clock into the sunlit hall and into the springtime outdoors. Thus, the style by which Mary Norton creates the details of setting is significantly related to tone and meaning, for the visual impressions, particularly of light and darkness, symbolize the characters themselves: Pod and Homily, nearsighted in their view of the world; Arrietty, yearning to escape the darkness to find realities to parallel her youthful visions.

Plot and characterization are developed around the action of the Clocks' being seen and the ways in which they react to seeing and being seen. Obviously, the family live by borrowing—in a sense, they live by seeing what has been left lying around, by perceiving its usefulness to them, and by gathering it without being seen, an occurrence that would require emigration to avoid capture. The plot can be divided into three sections, each of which centers on a major character being seen and contains a conflict as to whether or not the family should emigrate. In chapters 3 through 8, Pod's being seen by the boy threatens but does not totally disrupt the Clocks' lives; in chapters 9 through 14, Arrietty sees the boy and is later seen by her father while she talks to her new friend; and in chapters 15 through 18 the boy meets the entire family and fails in his attempt to carry them from the house after they have been seen by Mrs. Driver.

Appropriately, the direct narrative ends after the boy sees the Borrowers for the last time. Narrative and point of view are here linked, as his entrance into and departure from the lives of Pod, Homily, and Arrietty have precipitated the action of this momentous period of their lives. Although they have behaved in accordance with their basic personalities, he has been the catalyst acting on them, forcing them to emigrate, an action that may well have been inevitable. Not only does the action occur because he saw them, but also because of his relationship to them, the story has been related. But although the direct narrative of the Borrowers' lives concludes with chapter 18, the story is not over, for the boy continues to be an active force in their lives, courageously providing for what he believes to be their final escape, an event he never witnesses.

Who sees the Borrowers and how they react to them determine much of the meaning of the story. There are ten human beings, three of whom—the ratcatcher, the policeman, and the village boy—are of little importance except for the part they play in the final attempt to exterminate the Clocks and for the fact that all are skeptical of Mrs. Driver's sighting.

The four occupants of the house can be measured according to the extent of their belief in the reality of the Borrowers. Crampfurl does not believe, attributing all to the mischievousness of the boy and viewing Mrs. Driver's report with disdain. Great-Aunt Sophy thinks Pod is a product of her sherry drinking. While she does not literally believe, she has a kind of imaginative belief that renders her a more sympathetic character. She is close to Pod because, like him, she is a product of better days gone by. Mrs. Driver believes in what she sees, but her response is exaggerated and vindictive. She makes no attempt to understand the Borrowers and tells Crampfurl that she has discovered hundreds of little people. Appropriately, no one except the boy believes her, for hateful, vindictive liar that she is, she possesses neither sympathy nor understanding for the Clocks. The boy, of course, gradually develops these qualities of sympathy and understanding. His response to what he sees makes his summer with the Borrowers a turning point in his life.

The boy is also one of the three people who tell the story, and as such is part of the link in which point of view moves steadily from actual seeing of the Borrowers to imaginative insight. He is the appropriate link between the Clock family and his sisters, and through them, to Kate, for he not only views but understands. Mrs. May and Kate never see the Clocks, but do achieve strong imaginative insight. Perhaps the old woman's greatest achievement is her transmission of her imaginative sympathy and insight to Kate. Yet she never forces Kate to accept what she says, giving detail tentatively and, even at the end, casting some uncertainty over the story. It is as if she feels that the girl must come to a belief and faith based on her own understanding, her own insight. In Kate, she finds a receptive audience, the young girl liking the twilight sadness of the breakfast room and intuitively understanding, almost from the beginning, the details of the Borrowers' lives. By the end of the novel, Kate, who has never literally sighted a Borrower, has perhaps as complete a comprehension of Pod, Homily, and Arrietty as anyone else in the novel.

In essence, *The Borrowers* is about understanding and sympathy, about knowledge of self, and about insight into other people and beings. By seeing the story through the eyes of the boy and then Mrs. May and Kate, the reader is able not only to understand the central characters but also to trace the narrator's growing insight. As mentioned, a major concern is who earns the right to see the Borrowers. Crampfurl and Mrs. Driver do not, and it is fitting that no one believes the latter when she does. Great-Aunt Sophy has a partial right, and even she only partly believes her own eyes. The boy obviously has the right, and it is a tribute to him that Kate and Mrs. May later decide to retell his story and finish it for him. Their imaginative insight is stronger than Mrs. Driver's eyesight.

Stories Never Really End: Closure and the Necessity of Sequels

If chapters 19 and 20 create an emotionally and thematically satisfying closure to *The Borrowers*, and if the initial conflict of the Clock family between the need and reluctance to emigrate as a result of Pod's having been seen has been resolved, it must certainly have been apparent to early readers that there was more, "a lot more" (*Borrowers,* 158), to use Mrs. May's words, to be said about the Borrowers. What were the details of their lives after the escape, and did Arrietty, who had grown up so much in a few weeks, continue to mature? Readers must have expected that implicitly, Mary Norton, like Mrs. May, was making a promise: "I'm going to tell you" (*Borrowers,* 158). It seems probable that, writing as she was within the Nesbit tradition of several books about the same characters and having created a sequel to *The Magic Bed-Knob,* Mary Norton was leaving the door open for more by not providing verification for Mrs. May's accounts of the Clocks' arrival at a new home. One of the significant aspects of closure in children's fiction is the central characters' return to their own home or the establishment of a new and better one.[17] A sequel could possibly present such closure to the story of the Clock family.

Chapter Four
Stories Never Really End

The Borrowers Sequels

Early in *The Borrowers Afield*, Kate tearfully tells Tom Goodenough, the old gamekeeper from Firbank Hall, "I was only wondering . . . if they were all right . . . and how they managed . . . and whether they found the badger's set" (*Afield*, 30), no doubt echoing concerns for the Clock family felt by most readers of *The Borrowers*. Although the first book had achieved an aesthetically and thematically satisfying closure, much more happened—so much more that it took Mary Norton four more books to do the telling. In fact, these books can be seen not so much as a series of individual, although interconnected, novels as four volumes of one large work, tracing the stages of the Clocks' quest for a new home and Arrietty's growth to maturity. Midway in their trek across the fields in *The Borrowers Afield*, Pod tells Homily, "It's just that you don't *go back*, Homily, not once you've come out, you don't. And we ain't got a home. That's all over and done with. Like it or not, we got to go on now" (*Afield*, 124). Until they finally find a secure, safe home in the Old Rectory, the Clocks face a series of "evictions" and escapes, from an old boot and a discarded kettle, the interwall apartments they share with the Hendrearys at the gamekeeper's cottage, Vine Cottage in the model village of Little Fordham, and the attic room of their captors, the Platters. While all but the last seem initially to be homes, none is permanent. Interestingly, these unsuitable dwellings are either in the open or upstairs. At the Old Rectory, the Clocks will be on the ground floor for the first time since Firbank Hall.

From Home to Home: The Plots of the Sequels

The Borrowers Afield begins with an account of Kate's life in the year after she had learned about the Borrowers. Her interest in the story fades until Mrs. May invites her to travel to Bedfordshire, where the old woman has inherited a cottage, and tells her she will have an opportunity to see Firbank Hall. The first part of the visit is a disappointment to

Kate: the country inn is not so romantic as she had hoped, and Firbank Hall, nothing like what she had imagined. But when she meets Tom Goodenough, the aged occupant of the cottage, and learns that he had watched the attempted extermination of the Clocks, she turns the conversation toward the Borrowers. He gives her Arrietty's *Diary and Proverb Book,* shows her the entrance to their home in the old cottage, and in the ensuing days tells her all that Arrietty had told him about the family's escape from Firbank Hall, their travels across the fields, and their arrival at his home.

The Clocks' trek is not at all as Kate and Mrs. May had imagined at the conclusion of *The Borrowers.* After they have entered the field where they hope to find the badger-set home of their relatives, the Hendrearys, Pod transforms an abandoned boot into a temporary home. Their sense of security is short-lived, however, as, returning from a borrowing expedition, they discover that some of his tools are missing. They have been "borrowed" by Spiller, a half-wild Borrower boy who becomes their provisioner, bringing them cooked meat. When Pod finds the badger set, now inhabited by foxes, and no sign of the Hendrearys, the Clocks' situation changes dramatically. The boot must now become their home, and with winter approaching, their situation seems drastic. In despair, they go to bed for what they believe will be their last night on earth. The next morning, Arrietty discovers that the boot has been found by its former owner, Mild Eye the gypsy, and taken back to his caravan. Once again the Clocks are trapped, and this time with no apparent hope of a human being to rescue them. There is, however, a rescuer: Tom Goodenough, a friend of Spiller, who carries them to his cottage and takes them to a hole in the wall, which they enter. Climbing up a ladder, they arrive at the interwall apartment of the Hendrearys, where a joyous but somewhat strained reunion takes place. As the novel concludes, Arrietty sneaks from the apartment to the main house and begins a conversation with Tom.

The Borrowers Afloat also begins with a narrative framework. Mrs. May tells Mr. Beguid, her lawyer, the story of the Borrowers as she learned it from her brother in her childhood and more recently from Kate. Later, the girl and the woman peer into the mousehole through which the Clocks had passed on their way to the reunion with the Hendrearys. The direct narrative commences with a recounting of the reunion that had formed the concluding pages of *The Borrowers Afield.* Homily and Aunt Lupy barely get along, and Pod is enjoined from borrowing by Uncle Hendreary. Reduced to the status of totally dependent relations, Homily decides that the Clocks must leave. Their decision is finalized when Arrietty reports that Tom and his grandfather will be closing the cottage. But departure seems impossible, as Tom's escaped ferret hovers near their exit. At this point, Spiller returns and offers the Clocks both an avenue of escape—through a drainpipe to the riverbank—and a destination—Little Fordham, a model village. Although the family narrowly escape being washed away by a flood of bathwater from a tributary pipe, they arrive at the river and set up temporary housekeeping in an old kettle stuck in the bank. The kettle is dislodged from the bank by floods and spins wildly downstream until it is caught in a floating island of tangled branches, where the stranded family is discovered and nearly recaptured by Mild Eye. Once again, Spiller returns, and they travel to Little Fordham. The novel closes as Mrs. Driver and Crampfurl, the cook and gardener at Firbank Hall, sit in the kitchen discussing Mrs. Driver's encounter with the Borrowers. Crampfurl decides not to tell her that on his way home that evening, he had seen a tiny face peering from a toylike boat.

Although *The Borrowers Aloft* also begins with a discussion among human beings, there is a significant difference. The human beings are involved not merely with reconstruction of the central narrative but directly with the Borrowers' lives. Mr. Pott, a retired railway employee, is the builder of the model village. Miss Menzies is a lonely spinster who helps him, building tiny model figures for his layout. Mr. Platter is a businessman who has fallen on hard times and hastily erects a rival model village in the hope of luring customers to his wife's riverside teas.

The plot begins when the spying Mr. Platter, envious of the popularity of Mr. Pott's village, reports to his wife that the old railway man has "a lot of live ones,"[1] as well as his models, and decides that he and his wife must steal these to enhance their own business, which is again faltering. Meanwhile, Miss Menzies strikes up a friendship with Arrietty and leaves articles lying about for the Clocks to discover. The Clocks' happiness and security last only as long as the summer. One night after the close of the season, they are captured by the Platters, who imprison them for the winter in the attic of their home. The Borrowers learn that in the spring, they are to be exhibited in a glass-sided house in the Platters' model village. Hope comes when Arrietty, reading through a pile of *Illustrated London News* magazines, sees an article on ballooning and suggests that they leave their prison in a balloon. As time runs out, Pod, following instructions Arrietty reads to him, constructs a balloon from discarded objects found in the attic. It carries them to the edge of Little Fordham, where they find Spiller waiting for them in their home, which has been modernized and refurbished by Mr. Pott and Miss Menzies.

When Arrietty confesses that the comfort of their home is a result of her having been seen by and having talked with Miss Menzies, Pod announces that they must depart. The family decides to move to a mill run by a nearsighted old man, and Arrietty sadly promises never again to speak to human beings. The novel closes with an epilogue (which was dropped two decades later with the appearance of *The Borrowers Avenged*) in which the narrator announces that, as she has no further information about the Clock family, she can no longer continue telling the story. She does, however, offer hypotheses: Spiller and Arrietty will marry and later care for the aging Pod and Homily; Miss Menzies will care for Mr. Pott; and the Platters will move to a lower-class district of London.

But much more than that happened to the Platters, Miss Menzies, and the Clocks, all told in *The Borrowers Avenged,* which, like its predecessors, also begins from a human point of view. On 3 October 1911 (one of the few specific dates given to events of the five novels), Miss Menzies reports missing or possibly kidnapped persons to the kindly but disbelieving village constable and then visits the church, where she helps with the weekly arrangement of flowers. As she departs from the church, she appears skeptical of a friend's account of having heard a tiny voice in the kitchen. The implication, however, is clear to the reader: there are Borrowers in the church!

The next spring, the Platters sneak into Little Fordham to apprehend the escapees just as the Clocks depart for a new home: the semideserted rectory near the village church in which the Hendrearys have settled. Barely escaping, the family arrive safely at the rectory, where they begin to investigate possible locations for a permanent home, and Arrietty meets Peagreen, a lame Borrower living alone there.

On the Saturday before Easter, Mr. Platter and his wife go to the church to collect payment for work performed for a woman who is helping Miss Menzies decorate the church. The stage is set for the novel's climax. Arrietty's cousin Timmus is spotted by Mrs. Platter and barely escapes into a collection box, which is locked for the night. Later, the Platters, knowing where their prey is, break into the church and are discovered by Miss Menzies and the constable, who suspect them of attempted robbery. The next morning, Arrietty recounts the episode to Spiller and Peagreen and sobs that she had wanted to speak to Miss Menzies, who was frequently very near to her, but had refrained. She is comforted when Peagreen assures her that, having said he would do so,

Spiller will tell Miss Menzies of the family's safety, but not of their whereabouts. At the novel's close, Peagreen gently asks Arrietty if Borrowers are ever safe. A brief epilogue states that, although the fate of the Platters is unknown, they were never again seen by the Borrowers.

Echoes and Remembrances of Firbank Hall

Each of the four sequels, as well as the adventures in them, refers back to *The Borrowers.* The Clock home at Firbank Hall—run according to the time-honored rules and ethics of borrowing, but first to Arrietty and later to her parents increasingly unsuitable and dangerous—is the standard against which each of the temporary dwellings is measured. In addition, specific references to characters, actions, and objects of the first book, along with direct quotations and paraphrases from that book, serve to remind readers of the physical and psychological starting points of the Clocks' odyssey. By seeing where the family is coming from, readers can better understand not only its situation at different stages but also where it is going. They can also see how the second to fifth books in the series form a unified story, developing conflicts, character portrayals, and themes that achieve satisfying closure at the conclusion of *The Borrowers Avenged.*

The frame story of *The Borrowers Afield,* in which Kate and Mrs. May visit Firbank Hall, serves to reintroduce both Kate and the readers to the settings and characters of *The Borrowers,* to reestablish their faith in the existence of the characters, and to emphasize the pastness of that world, both to Kate and to the Clocks. Mrs. May, it is stated in words taken from the first book, "was, I think, some kind of relation" (*Afield,* 4), the person who taught Kate about crocheting and the Borrowers. Circumstantial evidence for the existence of Borrowers given in the first book—the list of safety pins, needles, blotting paper, and other items— is repeated. Arriving at Firbank Hall, Kate thinks about the human beings who had figured in the first story, realizing about Crampfurl "so there had been such a person" (*Afield,* 13), and later asking Tom Goodenough if he was the boy with the ferret. She is excited at seeing the grating, doorstopper, and front door, and at hearing the sound of the green baize kitchen door closing. Standing at the door, Kate stares at the stairs, "'going up and up, world upon world,' as Arrietty had described them [in *The Borrowers*]" (*Afield,* 17). She remembers the boy's reference to Arrietty's becoming "the last of her race" (*Afield,* 10). In a manner similar to her requests to Mrs. May in the first book, she begs Tom,

"Please! . . . let's go on about borrowers" (*Afield,* 27), and she is delighted to receive Arrietty's most prized possession, the *Diary and Proverb
Book,* from him. In conversations with Tom, she learns what she and
Mrs. May had only hypothesized about, the events after the Clocks'
escape.

Nonetheless, the physical world in which the Borrowers had lived has
been so altered as to exist now only in Kate's imagination, as it must also
for the Clocks. The stately mansion is a school, with a "barrack-y appearance" (*Afield,* 15): the gleaming floor is covered with linoleum; the clock
has been replaced with a radiator; the morning room is the headmaster's
study; and the kitchen is a lab. In the narrative she later creates for her
children, Kate makes little mention of Firbank Hall, focusing on the
fields and the gamekeeper's cottage, for, just as it became for the Clocks,
it has become past history for her.

In the direct narrative, the Clocks make few references to their past.
They are soon out of sight of Firbank Hall and have brought only a few
items from it—Arrietty's *Diary,* Pod's tools, and Homily's haircurlers
being the objects most frequently mentioned in *The Borrowers.* They
must adapt to the present if they are to have a future; their floorboard
house and its contents are conspicuous by their absence. When they
arrive at the Hendrearys, they discover that Aunt Lupy has some of the
items acquired during the golden age of borrowing that immediately
preceded their discovery by Mrs. Driver. But these look out of place
away from Firbank Hall.

Like the introductory frame narrative of *The Borrowers Afield,* that of
The Borrowers Aloft refers to the lost world of Firbank Hall, as Mrs. May,
in a situation paralleling that opening *The Borrowers,* introduces an out-
sider, Lawyer Beguid, to the subject of the Clock family. "They had
nothing of their own at all. Even their names were borrowed" (*Afloat*
13), she tells him, echoing her first explanation to Kate. Unlike Kate,
however, Mr. Beguid, like Mild Eye's wife and Crampfurl, is little
inclined to believe in their existence. Later, Mrs. May learns from Kate
that the Clocks had lived with the Hendrearys at the old cottage, but
had soon left. Just as Firbank Hall no longer belongs to Mrs. May's family and Tom Goodenough will have to vacate the gamekeeper's cottage,
so too have the Clocks had to leave their homes in both places. Living
with the Hendrearys is a reminder to them of all they have left behind.
The conversation between Mrs. Driver and Crampfurl at the conclusion
of *The Borrowers Afloat* is the last scene of the series set at Firbank. This
scene has the effect of closing the Clocks' life at Firbank.

In *The Borrowers Aloft,* the Clocks, imprisoned in the Platters' attic, are far from their old home Firbank, on the one hand, and from any secure new one, on the other. Not surprisingly, there are few references or echoes in this book of their lives as described in *The Borrowers.* Most of the references that do appear occur shortly after their capture, when, more vulnerable than ever before, they think back to the most secure residence they have known. Three sets of actions parallel those at Firbank, and these ominously foreshadow the Clocks' final departure from the model home at Little Fordham. Like the boy, Miss Menzies provides them with gifts; Mr. Pott removes the roof of Vine Cottage, leaving new furnishings for the family, as had been done with the kitchen floorboards at Firbank; and Homily, on their return to Vine Cottage, begins rearranging furniture, as she had during their golden age of borrowing. That time had been described as one "beyond all dreams of borrowing" (*Borrowers,* 130), while the refurbished Vine Cottage is referred to as "a home beyond their dreams" (*Aloft,* 183).

The epilogue to *The Borrowers Aloft,* which appears to close the series, includes the most extended parallels in the sequels with the language of *The Borrowers.* In the first book, when Kate had objected to Mrs. May's stopping of her narrative, the old lady had remarked that stories never really end: "They can go on and on and on. It's just that sometimes, at a certain point, one stops telling them" (*Borrowers,* 158). In the epilogue to *The Borrowers Aloft,* the narrator states: "Stories never really end. They can go on and on and on—and on: it is just that at some point or another the teller may cease to tell them" (*Aloft,* 192). To the reader very familiar with *The Borrowers,* there are hints that the story is not over at the end of *The Borrowers Aloft.* There are differences in the quoted parallel passages: the later one includes, after a dash, a fourth "and on"; the phrase "at a certain point" is changed to "at some point or another"; and "one stops" is changed to "the teller may cease." These changes suggest that the decision to stop is arbitrary. Moreover, one remembers that Mrs. May, after the statement she made, continued telling her story, bringing it, through guesswork, to an appropriate (if factually inaccurate) conclusion. The narrator of *The Borrowers Aloft* is in a similar position, needing guesswork and the reader's assistance to work out the conclusion. The Clocks' quest and the story's closure are not complete, despite the author's disclaimers, as this consideration of these parallels and differences implies.

The Borrowers Avenged contains more direct references to Firbank Hall, scenes that parallel those in *The Borrowers,* and phrases that paraphrase or quote directly from that book than are found in the three preceding volumes combined. The opening chapter, in which Miss Menzies reports the disappearance of the Clocks to the constable, provides a parallel to Mrs. May's first conversations with Kate. Like Mrs. May, she proceeds indirectly, using words almost identical to those of the old woman: "But you must have wondered about the mysterious way small objects seem to disappear. . . . [F]actories go on making needles and penpoints and blotting paper, and people go on buying them, and yet there never is a safety pin just when you want one, or the remains of a stick of sealing wax. Where do they all go to?" (*Avenged*, 9). The difference in this situation is that unlike Kate, who becomes so involved in what Mrs. May is talking about that she achieves an imaginative belief in the Clock family, the constable, who lives at the same time the Clocks do, is skeptical. He will not see them, let alone believe. The secret of their existence will not be known to the village, and from this quarter at least, they will be safe.

During their trip upriver with Spiller, Arrietty thinks about her life at Firbank, remembering her first trip beyond the floorboards; her first meeting and conversation with the boy, particularly his contention that "their race *was* dying out" (*Avenged*, 47); the time spent reading to him; and the knowledge she gained about the world of human beings. These reminiscences help to create a contrast between her life and personality as a child before the family's travels began and her current status as a young adult about to arrive at a new home. Exploring this home, the members of the family frequently compare it to Firbank as it was before they were seen by the boy. These references to their past life at Firbank, all of which was detailed in *The Borrowers*, serve to illustrate the superiority of the Old Rectory as a new home and to prepare readers for the end of the family's quest and the closure of their story.

Emigrés: *The Borrowers Afield*

Whereas *The Borrowers* had centered on the inevitability of the Clocks' having to leave their old home, *The Borrowers Afield* is about the search for a new and secure one. When the badger set is found abandoned, the Clocks view the boot as a home. Arrietty thinks of the riverbank location as "a kind of castle" (*Afield*, 82), although it will soon be seen to be much less secure than Pod's "fortress" (Borrowers, 13) beneath the floorboards. Pod creates clever devices for it; Homily begins sweeping and cleaning; and, as she brings Spiller for his first visit, Arrietty says of the boot, "it's our home" (*Afield*, 106). Yet as the invasions of a moth and mice indicate, it is vulnerable, and with no hope of reunion with the Hendrearys at the badger set and winter setting in, the Clocks' quest for a home seems to have failed. The warm gypsy caravan becomes a prison, and the tiny family is in danger of being placed in a bird cage and sold.

When at last they are safe and snug with the Hendrearys, deep within the walls of the gamekeeper's cottage, the Clocks' quest would seem to be fulfilled. But there is an uneasy peace. High above the floor, not beneath it, their new home is very different from their old. Hostilities between Homily and Aunt Lupy are barely suppressed. Arrietty's making contact with Tom Goodenough is the kind of action that had resulted in the family's forced evacuation from Firbank Hall. In a story about the search for a secure home, Mary Norton implicitly seems to be asking some unsettling questions. How long will this sense of security last? Will the Borrowers once again be forced to emigrate? While the plot achieves a fragile closure, it does not resolve the conflict between security and safety and danger and rootlessness. Arrietty's shy greeting to Tom Goodenough at the end of the book not only provides an explanation of how Tom learned of the events he reported to Kate but also suggests that this ending is more a respite from adventures than an end to them.

While the conclusion may be unsettling, many positive aspects of the adventure appear, particularly as they relate to the maturation process Arrietty had begun in the first book. Until the final chapter, Arrietty is in nature, active in an environment she had often gazed at longingly from her grating. How she reacts to this environment and the events that take place in it, especially compared with her parents' responses, will indicate the stages and extent of her growth toward adulthood. In many ways, her development follows the archetypal pattern feminist critic Annis Pratt has traced in female fiction (Pratt 1981, passim). Although Pratt maintains that truly fulfilled female development is seldom achieved and accordingly not depicted in women's novels, she believes one of the most vital and liberating aspects of a woman's life to be a time spent in a green world where the heroine becomes one with nature. An important aspect of this experience is an encounter with a green-world lover, a male who exists within the rhythms of nature and who is a counterpart and complement to her new sense of self. Unfortunately, Pratt argues, the benefits of this experience are generally destroyed as the woman accepts a limiting role in a male-dominated society.

Adrienne Rich's belief, quoted by Pratt, that "feminism . . . means finally that we renounce our obedience to the fathers and recognize that the world they have described is not the whole world"[2] is certainly revealed in the opening chapter of direct narrative. While Pod ostensibly maintains command of the exodus from Firbank Hall, several incidents subtly indicate that Arrietty is more responsible for the family's progress during the first day in the field: she shouts a warning about an approaching crow, notices threatening storm clouds, and discovers the abandoned boot. Recognizing the importance to Pod of his sense of control, however, she allows him to take credit for the discovery and praises him for saving the family from the bird. Significantly, she discovers the boot while walking alone, on higher ground above the family; she has a better, fuller view of the new world they are all entering.

The first to awaken the next morning, Arrietty explores the world around her: "This, Arrietty thought, is what I have longed for; what I have imagined: what I knew existed—what I knew we'd have" (*Afield,* 59). Although Arrietty, remembering the supposed fate of her cousin Eggletina, briefly wonders whether it was "really better, as her parents had always taught her, to live in secret darkness underneath the floor" (*Afield,* 60), she quickly rejects the thought and begins to climb a hedge, which, like the staircase at Firbank Hall, went "[u]p and up as far as she could see" (*Afield,* 60). She recognizes that she possesses the hereditary Borrower ability to climb, an ability that was repressed in her earlier life because she was a girl, not permitted to borrow. On her second excursion alone, she meets her "green-world lover," Spiller, the wild, orphaned Borrower. She is first disgusted at his dirtiness and shocked when she learns that he hunts and kills small game (mice), but her admiration and affection for him grows, and she finds herself defending him against her mother.

During the following weeks, her knowledge and love of the outdoors expand. Accommodation with nature and respect for the rights and differences of other creatures are important: "her world, she realized, was not their world and for them hers had little interest. . . . Benignity met with benignity: and anger, she found, was only aroused through fear" (*Afield,* 146). The apex of her green-world experience comes when she decks herself with flowers, pretending she is a fairy. She learns, however, that nature is not totally beneficent. Owls hunt at night and, given the opportunity, would quickly snatch her away. She must live on equal terms with her fellow creatures, as she realizes when she is nearly stung by a bee she traps inside a flower. Moreover, she must remain alert to dangers; her failure to do so results in a narrow escape, thanks to the vigilance of Spiller, from a marauding dog.

In discovering herself, Arrietty also learns to understand other people. She admires her mother's newfound courage, and at one point thinks that "she felt closer to Homily than she had felt for years—more like a sister, as she put it" (*Afield,* 75). While perceiving her father's limitations, she respects his knowledge and concern for his family, and although she disagrees with her parents, she knows not to push them. Even though Mild Eye is bent on imprisoning them, she feels sympathy for the gypsy when his wife mocks his report of sighting little people.

Arrietty's reaction to Spiller is most significant. With the exception of the boy at Firbank Hall, who is a member of a different species, Spiller is the first person of her own age she has ever met. Before she grows to love him, she must learn to respect him. In gender, background, and experience, he is everything she is not. Without parents, living in the open, he has had to develop his own code of ethics and means of survival. Arrietty's initial disgust and her anger at his method of rescuing her from the dog result in part from her immature attempts to judge him in terms of her own life. Still, as her reports to her mother about his background indicate, she has not only gathered many facts but has listened carefully in an attempt to understand him on his own terms. The extent of her success is partly indicated by her reactions to an overheard conversation about borrowing between the young man and her father: "This difference in approach was understandable, Arrietty thought. . . . Pod was a house-borrower, long established in traditional routine; whereas Spiller dealt exclusively with gypsies—here today and gone tomorrow—and must match his quickness with theirs" (*Afield,* 149). Just as her meeting with the boy had helped her to understand the difference between human beings and Borrowers, her encounters with Spiller assist her in comprehending two approaches to the occupation of borrowing. She is not using her father as the standard for judging another's competence. That she misses Spiller during his absences and is genuinely sorry that he has left the Hendreary apartments before she can thank him for their rescue indicates how important he has become to her. Different though he is in many ways, he is similar to her in his independence and love of freedom in nature.

Arrietty's actions and thoughts in the novel's final two episodes, the entrapment in and escape from Mild Eye's caravan and the arrival and reception at the Hendreary home, indicate how far she has come literally and symbolically since the family's trek began. After the first and last nights in the boot, Arrietty is the first to awaken. Whereas the first time she had joyously discovered freedom in nature, now she perceives the danger they are in. Later, she is forced to take control of the terrified Homily, repeatedly urging her mother to be quiet. Unlike her father, who would prefer imprisonment to being killed and eaten by the ferret they erroneously suppose to be in Tom Goodenough's pocket, Arrietty would prefer death to confinement. Brave, cautious, and determined, she is more self-possessed in the face of these dangers than her parents are. This may be symbolized by the fact that, as they travel in Tom Goodenough's pocket, she is the first member of the family to attempt standing on her own feet, something her independent friend Spiller is already doing.

Earlier in the novel, when Arrietty had thought reunion with the Hendrearys was close at hand, she had expressed joy. Now, as she mounts the ladder in the darkness, she is less certain. Her ascent is implicitly compared with her first climbing of the hedge. At that time, she had felt that "a ladder at best was a dull thing, whereas here was variety, a changing of direction, exploration of heights unknown" (*Afield,* 61). What lies at the top of the ladder does not provide Arrietty with the exhilaration found at the top of the hedge. The room, filled with many useless, decorative objects, seems unreal. Disheveled and dirty, she feels out of place; she anticipates quarrels between Homily and Lupy; and she feels a sense of confinement like that she had known beneath the floorboards. Alone out on the landing platform, she makes a momentous decision—to initiate for the first time a conversation with a human being, Tom: "If I don't do it now, she thought desperately, this first evening—perhaps, in the future, I should never dare again; there seemed too many rules in Aunt Lupy's house, too many people, and the rooms seemed too dark and too hot" (*Afield,* 213). The ambiguous feelings about security and freedom she had experienced beneath the floorboards at Firbank Hall are gone. As fears of confinement grow, she dares to break the fundamental rule of the Borrowers' code: avoidance of being seen by human beings. In doing so, she is asserting, however unconsciously, her rebellion against tradition and authority and her need for her own freedom.

During the novel, Arrietty experiences her most meaningful moments alone, away from her parents: climbing the hedge, she becomes fully aware of the wonder and expansiveness of nature; leaving Homily to gather nuts, she meets Spiller, whose character and life, so different from her family's, become increasingly attractive to her; leaving the boot beneath Mild Eye's bunk, she has a full understanding of the family's predicament; wandering from the Hendrearys' apartment, she rejects the known and secure for the uncertain, possibly dangerous encounter with a human being.

Unlike Arrietty, Pod and Homily neither experience the joy of nature nor learn a great deal from their adventures. Sheila Egoff has referred to their "well-defined, if static personalities,"[3] seeming to imply a certain limitation in Mary Norton's characterization of them. Rather, this static quality would seem to be a reflection of and perhaps even a comment on the limitations within the characters themselves. While both Pod and Homily show courage, resourcefulness, and a degree of adaptability to their new circumstances, they react essentially in terms of the mind-sets and values of their lives at Firbank Hall. Pod is the conservative, benevolent patriarch, laying down the law to his wife and daughter and seeking praise for domestic innovations that are not only his. Highly nervous, scolding and worrying, Homily is severely limited by her agoraphobia. She looks back with pride on her home, tries to make the boot a new home, and offers suggestions to Pod about how she would have arranged Mild Eye's caravan. Despite difficulties with Aunt Lupy, Homily experiences a great relief in arriving at a home that, even though new to her, provides a familiar, physically secure, enclosed environment.

Homily's relative inability to cope with the world beyond the floorboards can be interpreted as Mary Norton's implicit criticism of the negative effects of a patriarchal system of marriage. As noted in the discussion of *The Borrowers*, Homily had once told Arrietty of her youthful joy at briefly escaping her claustrophobic environment to explore the house and, occasionally, the outdoors. Now that Homily is in the outdoors, she cannot respond joyfully, as Arrietty does. Her life with Pod, defined by a gender-based division of labor that has kept her in the house and dependent on her husband, has destroyed her adventurous, wondering capacities. Pod too has been imprisoned by his role, one in which his activities are circumscribed both physically and psychologically. He and his wife are static because they are no longer able to change; unlike Arrietty, they lack the ability to be influenced positively by the brave new world in which they are "afield."

Spiller, by contrast, has no tradition within which to define himself. A product of the wilderness rather than of the ordered, stratified world of Firbank Hall, he is somewhat like the gypsy Mild Eye, a vagabond living on the edges of society, responsible to and for no one else. Asked by Arrietty about his place of residence and his age, he replies vaguely, not only because of his cautionary evasiveness but also because he has not defined himself as a person. In fact, he does not have a real name, having mistaken a remark his mother had made about his eating habits—she had said he was a dreadful spiller—as his name. In many ways, he is like James Matthew Barrie's Peter Pan, a motherless, self-centered, somewhat amoral boy with no sense of family ties. Socially immature and irresponsible, he speaks little, has no scruples about borrowing weapons from Pod, and has little understanding of Arrietty's love of play. Yet he is a survivor. Because he is a part of nature, able to blend into the foliage, he can provide for himself and, later, for the Clock family. He never loses his wildness, but he does become somewhat domesticated and socialized, partly by Homily's fussing ministrations but mainly through his growing affection for the family, especially Arrietty. His attachment and concern lead to his seeking Tom's aid to rescue them from Mild Eye and then to his adopting a protective attitude when Tom becomes overly curious about them. Spiller represents the direction toward which Arrietty's maturation process is taking her, although because of her sense of family and tradition, she will never become the creature of the wilderness he is.

Unlike *The Borrowers, The Borrowers Afield* focuses little on human beings. Although the actions of Mrs. Driver are responsible for their situation, the members of the Clock family do not encounter any human beings until near the end of the novel, when they are seen first by Mild Eye, who has inadvertently brought them into his caravan; then by his skeptical wife; and finally by Tom Goodenough. They do attempt to avoid being seen by human beings, but their main efforts are directed toward surviving in an inhospitable and often dangerous natural landscape. Their encounters, however, echo those of *The Borrowers*. Tom Goodenough, like Mrs. May's brother, is helpful and sympathetic, while Mild Eye is destructive, considering for them a fate worse than death: imprisonment and exhibition. Mild Eye is also like Mrs. Driver in that his sighting is not believed by others.[4] These three characters reveal the ever-present danger of and necessity for human beings on the part of the Borrowers. Even young Tom is both a help and a danger, for while he takes them to their new home, he also seems to view them as possessions, remarking, "I reckon I got the best collection of borrowers in two counties" (*Afield,* 197).

Tom's proprietary interest in the Clocks and Hendrearys is one manifestation of an important theme introduced in *The Borrowers,* examined in *The Borrowers Afield,* and explored most fully in *The Borrowers Aloft* and *The Borrowers Avenged:* the nature of and interrelationship between borrowing, stealing, possession, and ownership. In *The Borrowers,* the boy

had called Pod's activities stealing and was puzzled by Arrietty's defini-
tion of stealing as the action of one Borrower taking from another. But
later, he tells Mrs. Driver that he is not a thief but a borrower. Mrs.
Driver, who regularly takes Aunt Sophy's sherry, considers herself not a
thief but someone taking as a right of her profession. The difference
between stealing and borrowing appears to be a matter of need and
motivation. That is why, in *The Borrowers Afield,* Homily is finally able to
forgive Spiller's taking of the hat pin and half-scissors. Although he has
broken the primary ethic that the Borrowers never borrow from another
Borrower, his need has been as great as the Clocks', and he has used
Pod's tools to help him supply many of their needs. Similarly, Mild Eye's
theft of one pair of boots is not condemned as thievery, for he had
greater need than the rich person, who owned many pairs. Mild Eye's
sense of ownership of the Borrowers is wrong, however; they are people
who cannot be owned and exploited. Thus, Tom's theft of them from
Mild Eye is justified: he wishes not to own them but to free them, even
though he does, in a way, view them as his. Finally, the overfurnished
Hendreary apartment, stocked with many useless, unfunctional items,
including an imitation leg of mutton, indicates that possession without
need is foolish. (It will be remembered that the Clocks' possession of
many of these items, once borrowed by the boy to feed Homily's house-
pride, had led to their being discovered by Mrs. Driver.)

The examination of the nature of ownership and possession is carried
over into the frame story, as are many of the other themes of *The
Borrowers Afield.* Tom Goodenough, like the Borrowers, is about to be
dispossessed. Legal documents, written in a language Kate finds incom-
prehensible, will force him to leave the house he has lived in for more
than 80 years. While it is plain and dirty in the eyes of Lawyer Beguid
(who is an Olympian, like Mrs. Driver), the thatch, as Kate notices, is in
good repair. Goodenough has worked and is still working at keeping a
good roof over his head. Ironically, he is to be sent to an almshouse, to
become a Borrower for his remaining days. Just as the Hendrearys had
taken possession of Homily's furniture, Mrs. May, who had lived as a
kind of Borrower in Kate's house, is possessing Tom's house.

Beguid refers to Tom as "[t]he biggest liar in five counties" (*Afield,*
20). No doubt his reputation was earned because the villagers, like
Crampfurl and Mild Eye's wife, had not believed people who said they
had seen Borrowers. Yet what he had told the villagers was true; he had,
through his conversations with Arrietty, come to know and understand
his tiny tenants as well as the boy had. And as was the case with the boy,

his encounters with Arrietty had influenced his character. Curious and possessive at first, he had become a friend to Arrietty, filling in his lonely evenings as the other boy had his days, listening to her accounts of her family's life and adventures.

He is also the link between the framework and the inner narratives. Before she meets him, Kate's knowledge of the Clock family had been based on thirdhand knowledge—from Arrietty to the boy, to Mrs. May, and then to her—and on speculation. Now she meets someone who has actually talked with a Borrower and possesses "hard" evidence: Arrietty's *Diary and Proverb Book.* Her reaction to her new information and the way this leads to her writing down Arrietty's story many years later provide the focal point of the first four chapters of the novel.

In the year after she and Mrs. May had first talked about the Borrowers, "the story . . . became pushed away in the back of Kate's mind with other childish fantasies" (*Afield,* 5).[5] When Mrs. May talks about going to Bedfordshire, Kate's replies are vague and polite. Nevertheless, her attitude quickly changes to eagerness. The desire to believe surges within her as she asks Mrs. May, "on a note of anguish, 'You did believe in them, didn't you? Or was it . . . only a story?'" (*Afield,* 7). During the next few days and in the years that follow, she sifts the evidence. The process, however, involves a great deal of revising, for as the opening words of chapter 2 state, "nothing turns out in fact as you have pictured it" (*Afield,* 11). Kate must use her imagination to envision the past. The scene of such wonderful adventures, Firbank Hall is now a school; only the shoescraper, the grating (repaired), the staircase, and the green baize door remain unchanged. Looking at the open front door, she realizes that it was that way "years ago on that never-to-be-forgotten day for Arrietty when she first saw the 'great-outdoors'" (*Afield,* 13). Called by Mrs. May when she has run around the corner to see the grating, she thinks of Pod's call to Arrietty. And viewing the stairs, she remembers how Arrietty had described them. Significantly, Kate, the young girl, is perceiving the world as she imagines Arrietty would have done. This perception is the first major step she makes on the way to re-creating Arrietty's story for her own children.

Kate's quest for knowledge and belief continue during her meetings with Tom Goodenough. The old man, like Coleridge's Ancient Mariner, is immediately attracted to Kate, almost as though he sees in her the appropriate recipient of his story. She cleverly and subtly moves the conversation toward a discussion of the Borrowers, mentioning things she had learned from Mrs. May. Although he tries to redirect the conversation, speaking of field mice and badgers, she persists, prying from him the facts that he was the boy with the ferret and that he knows what happened to the Clocks after their escape. When his refusal to divulge his information causes Kate to weep profusely, in a manner similar to her crying late in *The Borrowers,* he produces Arrietty's *Diary and Proverb Book.* After Tom shows Kate the Gothic-shaped hole behind the wood-pile, Kate begins the process of revising the story she and Mrs. May created a year earlier. Just as the inn and Firbank Hall had not been what she expected, neither had the fate of the Borrowers. Tom, she realizes, had met Arrietty, who had told him about all the events. That night, back at the inn, reading Arrietty's tiny book, she devises her plan: "she would ask Tom to explain the headings [Arrietty's brief notations]. . . . And this was, more or less, what did happen" (*Afield,* 38).

Kate's need to know and believe, as well as her growing friendship with Tom, explains the source of the central narrative. It does not explain the reasons for her writing it down years later for her children, even though she promises Tom that she will not. In doing so, she is providing them with a link to her childhood past and through it to the lives of beings whose existence most human beings denied. Tom repeats to Kate Arrietty's observation that "[i]t's so awful and sad . . . to belong to a race that no sane person believes in" (*Afield,* 173). The writing is also an act of homage to her friend Tom. Everyone had laughed at him as a great liar, and "it was this thought which, long after she was grown up, decided Kate to tell the world" (*Afield,* 38–39). Both the telling and the tale are affirmations of the value of the lives of Tom and the Clocks and of the importance of sympathetic, imaginative understanding of the past.

The novel's opening paragraph also notes that Kate "compiled it as you compile a case-history or a biographical novel from all kinds of evidence—things she remembered, things she had been told and one or two things, we had better confess it, at which she just guessed. The most valuable piece of evidence was a miniature Victorian notebook" (*Afield,* 3). Significantly, this is an act of interpretation. Given the facts (the notebook and Tom's responses) the adult Kate is able to create the account of the outer and, more important, inner maturation of Arrietty to give to her children, who are also growing. This act of homage to Tom and Arrietty is also a gift to her children and a tribute to her sensitivity as an adult. She has not become an Olympian like Mrs. Driver, Mild Eye's wife, or Lawyer Beguid.

Mrs. May had told Kate, "Anything we haven't experienced for ourselves sounds like a story. All we can ever do is sift the evidence" (*Afield,*

8). In the English edition, this sentence reads, "All we can ever do about such things is . . . keep an open mind and try to sift the evidence."[6] Because she has been able to do both, Kate has been able to transform a story, in the sense of a narrative not considered to be factual, into something true and worthy of belief. She can pass on the story and presumably her belief to her children. This is what the third-person narrator of the opening chapter (Mary Norton herself, perhaps) does for the readers of the book. In the last sentence of the fourth chapter, she writes, "Let us sift the evidence ourselves" (*Afield,* 39). Just as Kate has used her abilities as a sensitive, sympathetic listener to help her become an active re-creator of the story, so too are readers urged not to be passive, but to use actively what they read as the basis on which to build their own responses.

The framework of the story is thus an integral part of the novel's meaning. It assists readers in the achievement of a willing suspension of disbelief. Kate provides distance necessary to enhance an aura of mystery and wonder essential to fantasy. Through her link to Tom Goodenough, she also provides an element of plausibility to the narrative; she had met someone who had known a Borrower, the one she herself was most interested in. More important, the frame reinforces the themes of the inner story. Kate's growth parallels Arrietty's; the Clocks' displacement is not unlike Tom's; Lawyer Beguid's discussion of property and ownership relates to the ethics of borrowing, stealing, and possession. Moreover, the Borrowers' ability to adapt imaginatively found objects to new, valuable uses parallels that of Kate with her sources and that which the third-person narrator expects of her readers.

Drifting: *The Borrowers Afloat*

The Borrowers Afloat continues the theme of a quest for a home presented in *The Borrowers Afield*. Initially filled with a "sense of security—the natural joy a borrower feels when safely under cover" (*Afloat,* 24), the Clocks realize that they have not reached their goal; life with the Hendrearys offers neither the comfort nor the contentment for which they had longed. Once again, emigration into the outdoors, into the natural world filled with terrors and dangers, is necessary. The fate of their temporary abode, the kettle, spinning down the flooded stream, emphasizes their continuing insecurity. Although they are last viewed moving toward the much-desired Little Fordham, the fact that they have been seen by Crampfurl, one of the Olympian human beings of *The Borrowers,* implicitly raises doubts about the safety they will enjoy on their arrival.

Is the quest ever to be fulfilled, or will they merely enjoy a brief respite before they face new and possibly greater dangers?

Arrietty's reactions to the experiences at the Hendrearys and while afloat reveal her continuing character growth. There are, however, some surprising changes in the way Homily reacts to the same circumstances. Pod's character remains static, although there is a sense of his loss of status as the captain of his family, for Uncle Hendreary places strict limitations on his borrowing activities, activities that are psychologically necessary for his sense of self-worth, and he is dependent on Spiller's ingenuity for their escape from both the house and Mild Eye and for their transportation to Little Fordham.

At the beginning of the direct narrative of *The Borrowers Afloat*, Arrietty feels imprisoned in the dark, cloistered apartment between the walls. She spends much of her time thinking of Spiller, worrying that the family has not thanked him for rescuing them, and is eager for his return. Her response indicates that she is maturing, considering him, probably unconsciously, as a possible mate. Significantly, he reminds her of the world of nature: "To talk of Spiller reminded her of out-of-doors and of a wild, free life she might never know again" (*Afloat,* 46). He has indeed become Annis Pratt's green-world lover, a male who symbolizes freedom from a conventionalized, repressive, patriarchally dominated life. Arrietty recognizes that "[t]his new-found haven among the lath and plaster had all too soon become another prison" (*Afloat,* 46). Her one regret is leaving the youngest Hendreary boy, Timmis, to whom she has become a kind of mother.

The story she tells Timmis a few days before the family leaves is significant. At her mother's suggestion, she discusses Little Fordham, the model village that "had become a kind of legend to borrowers" (*Afloat,* 65): "Arrietty went on, and on—explaining and inventing, creating another kind of life. Deep in this world she forgot the present crisis, her parents' worries and her uncle's fears, she forgot the dusty drabness of the rooms between the laths, the hidden dangers of the woods outside and that already she was feeling rather hungry" (*Afloat,* 66–67). Her account (which indicates that Mary Norton had already begun to plan *The Borrowers Aloft*) provides another example of the importance in the series of storytelling—for both the tellers and the listeners. Not only does it provide entertainment for Timmis and imaginative escape from a dreary environment for both of them, but also it gives Arrietty the opportunity of envisioning a place that provides protection without the confinement of her present and past dwellings. Her telling seems to have been influenced by the "relief and joy" (*Afloat*, 65) she has just experienced on learning that her parents have decided to leave the gamekeeper's cottage. Her earlier narratives to Mrs. May's brother and Tom Goodenough were retrospective, describing and explaining for both herself and her listeners aspects of her own and her family's past. Now, for the first time she is developing a story about what, it turns out, will become a future home. As part of her maturation process, she is creating a narrative that may well provide a framework within which to organize and understand the next stages of her life.

The escape down the dark tunnel is a joyous experience for Arrietty, "leading as it did toward a life to be lived away from dust and candlelight and confining shadows—a life on which the sun would shine by day and the moon by night" (*Afloat*, 104–5). After the bathwater flood, "Arrietty . . . felt somehow purged as though all traces of the old dark, dusty life had been washed away" (*Afloat*, 113). Moving from the tunnel into the sunlight of a springtime dawn and the world of nature is a kind of symbolic rebirth.

Critics have been relatively unsympathetic toward Homily's character as it is revealed in her reactions to the sojourn at and departure from the Hendrearys'. Nigel Hand, for one, remarks that "in the character of Homily . . . we are shown the dangers of petulance and regression" (Hand, 51). Homily is frequently fussy, finicky, and flustered, worried about being seen in her red petticoat, concerned about the slime of the drainpipe and the dirtiness of the kettle, and prone to muttering, "Oh, my goodness" (*Afloat*, 135) during the initial stages of a crisis. Pod, however, is aware of the character strengths she possesses, strengths to which these critics have paid scant attention. As the family sits in the main room of the deserted cottage, all escape routes apparently blocked, he tells Arrietty, "There's two kinds of courage I know of, . . . and your mother's got both of 'em" (*Afloat*, 85–86). He does not elaborate. However, he seems to be referring to Homily's ability to face the reality of the situation the family finds itself in and to "bury our pride" (*Afloat*, 83), a quality she highly values, in the interests of Arrietty's survival. With escape from the cottage apparently impossible, she is willing to return to the Hendrearys and beg for their assistance. During their precarious life afloat, she thinks less of herself than of Pod. When he refuses a place in the soapbox boat, she takes his jacket from him: "She folded it gently across her knees and patted it soberly as though . . . it were tired, like Pod" (*Afloat*, 107). And during the bathwater flood, she reaches out to hold his hand as he stumbles. She puts a bright face on the nearly disastrous incident, remarking, "Sandalwood! . . . Your father's favorite soap" (*Afloat,* 111), and seems pleased that the soaking has cleaned their clothes. Rather than pine for her lost home, she tells Pod that, more than a gold ring, "I'd sooner [have] a safety pin . . . living as we do now" (*Afloat,* 124). Trapped on the floating island, she observes that things could be much worse and announces that she could even eat a worm. Her attitude to Spiller has changed: no longer is he the dirty boy who is to be considered only when he has been of service to them. She is genuinely chagrined when she tells Arrietty that she had not thanked him.

After their rescue, she makes a statement she could not have made before: "maybe there is always some way to manage. The trouble comes, like—or so it seems to me—in whether or not you hit on it" (*Afloat,* 186). She is last seen admiring her husband's new apparel, the white summer suit donated by Spiller. Homily's situation is much different from that of Mrs. Driver, whose conversation with Crampfurl closes the novel. Nestled into the sheep's wool in Spiller's boat, she feels secure and contented as she and her family travel to their new home. Mrs. Driver, living in a house she does not own, must face the taunts of Crampfurl, and responds both angrily and wearily. She will never enjoy the sense of family and communication that Homily experiences. Like Bilbo Baggins, J. R. R. Tolkien's symbol of ordinary English people who showed great courage in times of crisis, Homily acts admirably during this stage of the family's journey. Perhaps the spirit of adventure she had enjoyed as a youth is reemerging after having been repressed for so many years.

The Borrowers Afloat is the last novel in the series to use a narrative framework to introduce the account of the Clock family's adventures. As noted, the frameworks of *The Borrowers* and *The Borrowers Afield* traced the methods by which Kate and Mrs. May had re-created the main story and related to themes within it. The framework for *The Borrowers Afloat* is markedly different. It emphasizes that events may have been quite different from the imaginative re-creation of them. The frame ends as Mrs. May tells Kate that she "can imagine what Homily felt, homeless and destitute, faced with that dusty hole. . . . And strange relations living up above who didn't know she was coming and whom she hadn't seen for years" (*Afloat,* 23). The next sentence, however, the opening one of chapter 2, undercuts the validity of the old woman's surmises: "But Mrs. May was not quite right: she had underestimated their sudden sense of security" (*Afloat,* 24).

With an awareness of Mrs. May's own situation, first living with Kate's family and now about to have her own home, readers can perceive how subjective her response is, just as Kate's must have been reconstructing Arrietty's adventures in *The Borrowers Afield.* Not that imaginative reconstruction is wrong in itself—the Clock family continue to live, 50 years after their adventures, because they are remembered by Mrs. May and Kate. Still, individuals cannot truly or fully understand other people, no matter how sympathetic they may be. This may be a reason for Mary Norton's switch to an omniscient, third-person narrator. There is no indication that the narrative that follows is based on information acquired or surmises made by Kate or Mrs. May. The existence of the Clock family has been almost definitely established by the *Diary and Proverb Book* now possessed by Kate. Moreover, they have been seen by another human being: Crampfurl. Although Norton may have planned to include him in the next book, she did not; however, the fact that someone to whom Kate could have had no access has seen them confirms finally and firmly the reality of their having existed. The focus can now be directly on their lives and their interrelationships with human beings.

The second encounter with Mild Eye and the sighting by Crampfurl reintroduces a major theme of *The Borrowers,* one to be treated more fully in the last two books of the series: how people who see the Borrowers react to them, and how these reactions influence the insecure lives of the tiny people. The conversation between Mrs. May and Lawyer Beguid that takes up most of chapter 1 also serves as a kind of commentary on the human beings who contact the Borrowers. Lawyer Beguid, hiding behind legal language, is openly skeptical about them and about those who believe. He considers Tom Goodenough a no-good humbug; Kate, an annoying and at best curious child; and Mrs. May, a member of a family he had long considered odd. Although mildly interested in Mrs. May's discussion, he erroneously refers to the Borrowers as "cadgers" (*Afloat,* 13). The term is significant, for in referring to them as beggars, he links them to Tom Goodenough, for whom he has little use. Interestingly, when the two adults return to the cottage, he looks in but does not cross the threshold. Literally and symbolically, he is unable to enter the realm of the Borrowers; he lacks both the sympathy and the imagination to believe and understand. He is like Crampfurl in *The Borrowers* and Mild Eye's wife in *The Borrowers Afield.* Mrs. May, on the other hand, is at the point of recovering her belief. She is somewhat embarrassed and shy as she talks to the lawyer about "[t]he family we knew" (*Afloat,* 13). Guided by Kate, a true believer, to the tiny opening behind the woodpile, she regains her faith. Like Tom Goodenough and, later, Miss Menzies, both of whom actually see the Clocks, she not only believes, but she sympathizes with them and their plight.

During her talk with Lawyer Beguid, Mrs. May has been inspecting renovations to the cottage she owns and will soon take possession of. Yet she does not view ownership as solely hers, for she intends to will the property to Kate. It is something to be shared, as her story had been. As such, her attitude is in contrast to that of Aunt Lupy and Mild Eye. Aunt Lupy had made the point clear that she was only lending household articles to the Clocks, and when the gamekeeper and Tom leave, she piously announces, "I don't want to seem hard, Homily, but in times like these, it's each one for his own" (*Afloat*, 69–70). Mild Eye, a poacher illegally catching others' fish, wishes to capture the Borrowers so that, possessing them, owning them, he can acquire riches for himself. Finally, Mrs. May's joy in having her own home can be compared with that of Homily as she anticipates the arrival at Little Fordham.

Model Tenants: *The Borrowers Aloft*

The Borrowers Aloft continues the examination of Arrietty's character development, particularly her relationship with Spiller. Homily, most notably during her time of domestic happiness, behaves much as she did in *The Borrowers*. Pod, during their imprisonment, is once again the patriarchal authority figure. Spiller remains as shadowy and evasive as ever and is seen mainly through the eyes of the Clocks. What makes the novel markedly different from the earlier three is the greater attention given to the human beings who affect the Borrowers' lives. Indeed, an important theme of *The Borrowers Aloft* is the complex and delicate interrelationships between the Clocks and these human beings.

In discussions with Mr. Pott during the Clocks' early days at their new home, Miss Menzies describes an incident that symbolizes Arrietty's character development during the novel: "Spiller found a chrysalis, which he gave to Arrietty. She kept it until last week. It turned out to be a red admiral butterfly. She watched it being born. But when its wings appeared and they began to see the size of it, there was absolute panic. Just in the nick of time, they got it out of the front door" (*Aloft*, 46). Fifteen when the novel begins, Arrietty spends much of their winter of imprisonment like a chrysalis, dormant. During their escape and after their return to Little Fordham, she emerges as an adult, leaving behind her childhood and its confinements as she develops a clearer understanding of her relationship with Spiller and of her place in the Borrower scheme of life.

While Pod and Homily are happy in their new home, Arrietty is not. She snaps rudely at her father's command to be still in front of Miss Menzies: "Stillness, stillness, quiet, quiet, creep, creep, crawl, crawl. . . . What's the good of being alive?" (*Aloft,* 48). Pod attributes her attitude to what he calls "the awkward age" (*Aloft,* 48), and he may be partly right. Her missing Spiller may be one of the causes. Arrietty has been thinking of how she had enjoyed riding on the model train and exploring with Spiller, "and when Spiller was not there, Arrietty was often lonely" (*Aloft,* 50). More important, she feels guilty about concealing her friendship with Miss Menzies from her father. She wonders about the longing "which drew her so strongly to human beings" (*Aloft,* 49). In addition, as she matures she may need to experience the world in relation to adults other than her mother and father. Just as her restlessness had led to a friendship with the boy at Firbank Hall and later with Tom Goodenough, it now leads to Miss Menzies. Miss Menzies is an adult, nonfamily female companion so frequently important to adolescent girls. The boy had described the larger world from a male child's point of view, focusing on pageants and sporting events. In recounting her life to the girl, the older woman exposes Arrietty to other aspects of this larger world: London social engagements and male companionship. Arrietty learns about the precariousness of relationships as she hears about Miss Menzies's cousin's marriage to another woman, and exclaims, "I think he ought to have married you!" (*Aloft,* 56). As she listens, Arrietty hypothesizes about a relationship with Spiller: "what fun it would have been to go riding with Spiller, as Miss Menzies had gone riding with Aubrey" (*Aloft,* 56).

During the winter spent in the Platters' attic, Arrietty seems to withdraw. When they are deposited on the floor, she clings to her father in fear, showing none of the exhilaration, curiosity, or courage she had exhibited during the moments before the flight from Firbank Hall or in Mild Eye's caravan. She meekly accepts Pod's assertion of leadership, takes little part in family conversations, and walks "listlessly" (*Aloft,* 100) over copies of the *Illustrated London News.* Arrietty, during this winter of discontent, has entered a period of withdrawal or dormancy that psychologists such as Bruno Bettelheim have seen as an important phase of female adolescence and that in folktales has been symbolized by sleep or death, as in the case of Sleeping Beauty or Snow White.[7] Yet this withdrawal period, or chrysalis stage, is in no way a death, for within the adolescent changes are occurring that allow her to emerge a young adult. These are indicated by Arrietty's changing response to her reading. She becomes "immersed" (*Aloft,* 110) in articles about ballooning,[8] and then she breaks away from her reading to offer her suggestion of escape by balloon. Spring has come, and Arrietty has reemerged into the world, bringing new ideas that will enable them to leave their prison. She has redefined her position in her family and her relationship with her parents.

After this, Arrietty takes a more active role in the escape plan than she had in the family's previous escapes. She reads and rereads the ballooning articles to her father, finds the large toy balloon they need, and suggests that an old music box be used as part of the process. She also thinks of Spiller, something she had not done during the winter, imagining how skillfully he would have worked at assembling this balloon and wishing he "could have seen the first attachment of the basket by raffia bridles to the load ring" (*Aloft,* 143). She believes his presence would have prevented Homily from making what was a nearly disastrous mistake during a test flight.

Although Arrietty, like the admiral butterfly, has escaped from a confining house, her journey toward maturity is not yet complete. She must understand more clearly her relationships with Spiller and her family. As she thinks of how much her friend would enjoy the balloon flight, she announces, just as she realizes it herself, "When I grow up, I think I'll marry Spiller" (*Aloft,* 152). She tells her mother that the two of them share a love of the outdoors and, recalling the sadness of Miss Menzies's love life, decides she must tell the shy Spiller of her intentions before he marries someone else. When Homily comments that they are more like brother and sister, she remarks that "this seemed quite a good kind of trial run for what was after all a lifelong companionship" (*Aloft,* 153). But the reunion with Spiller does not go as smoothly as she had hoped. She is upset that the balloon collapses before he has a chance to see it and that he appears more interested in talking to Pod than to her. She seems to be reverting to childish behavior, wanting Spiller to focus his attention on her and to praise her for her role in the construction and flying of the balloon. Only at the end of the novel, when he says he will inform Miss Menzies of the family's safety, does she realize the depth of his interest in her.

Arrietty perceives the nature of her status as a Borrower after she tells her family and Spiller that she had seen and talked to Miss Menzies. The motivations for her confession are complex: she is angry at being ignored by her mother, father, and Spiller as they sit around the hearth; she feels they should know of and appreciate her part in the refurbishing of their home; and she is relieving herself of the guilty burden of concealment. Another motive may exist, one she is unconscious of. In *The Borrowers,* she had learned that once having been seen, Borrowers must emigrate. Perhaps if she tells her father of her friendship with Miss Menzies, they will have to move from this place where they must stay indoors all day to avoid being seen by the many tourists. What she learns from her father after the confession is that, no matter how well intentioned, human beings will ultimately cause harm to Borrowers; that when Borrowers are seen by human beings, they run the danger of being treated like pets and enslaved; and that "making your own way . . . is what counts" (*Aloft,* 187). Because being given things rather than borrowing them robs Borrowers of independence, her actions can lead only to her losing the freedom she so earnestly desires. Finally, Pod talks to Arrietty of her future responsibility as an adult Borrower: "Say, someday, you had a little place of your own. A little family maybe—supposing, like, you'd picked up a good borrower. D' you think you'd go making up to humans? Never . . . . And I'll tell you for why: you wouldn't want to do nothing to put that family in danger. Nor that borrower either" (*Aloft,* 189–90). A fulfilled adult life with Spiller and a family can be achieved only by completely dissociating herself from human beings. By giving her promise never to speak to another human being, Arrietty reveals that she has taken an adult perspective. Her bildungsroman, which began with her gazing longingly through the grating in *The Borrowers,* appears to have been completed.

Pod's delineation of the dangers human beings present to Borrowers relates to a central theme of *The Borrowers Aloft:* the attitudes that human beings have toward Borrowers they see. Some are helpful and ultimately sympathetic; others are threatening and potentially destructive. By focusing the first five chapters of *The Borrowers Aloft* on the characters and lives of the Platters, Mr. Pott, and Miss Menzies, Norton directs the reader's attention to this theme.

Mr. Pott and Mr. Platter are characterized by their attitudes toward their respective model villages. Little Fordham, a detailed replica of the nearby town, was painstakingly constructed over several years when Mr. Pott had retired from the railroad after losing his leg rescuing a badger from an approaching train: "Mr. Pott was a good man, very kind and gentle. He loved his fellow creatures almost as much as he loved his trains" (*Aloft,* 12). Although they are a nuisance, he willingly lets children view his village and asks only that adults who accompany them donate a penny to the Railway Benevolent Fund. All who wish to do so are free to take "a glass of cool water" (*Aloft,* 24) as they pass through his kitchen. The local blacksmith and stonemason gladly help him in his construction projects. In contrast, business losses impel Mr. Platter to build his village. Learning of the popularity of Mr. Pott's model village, he "whipped [one] up in no time at all" (*Aloft,* 23). After each lessening of business of the riverside teas, he hastily duplicates Mr. Pott's attractions, charging higher admission fees with each renovation.

The existence of the Borrowers in Little Fordham is known to both Mr. Platter and Mr. Pott. In keeping with their characters and their attitudes toward their respective villages, their responses to the Clock family are different. Mr. Platter, who has discovered the Clock family while spying to discover Mr. Pott's latest inventions, views them as a threat to his business. When he informs his wive of their existence, she decides that "these . . . whatever they are" (*Aloft,* 65) must be stolen and used as the star attraction at Ballyhoggin, as they call their place. Before they undertake the kidnapping expedition, Mr. Platter begins to view the Clocks as objects and property, announcing, "They *are* part of the stores in a manner of speaking" (*Aloft,* 66).

Mr. Platter's intense, economic interest in the Borrowers is in contrast to Mr. Pott's vague interest in Miss Menzies's enthusiastic accounts of the tiny girl she has befriended. More concerned with work on the model railroad, he listens mainly to humor a woman whom, a "talker" (*Aloft,* 34) like his late wife, he likes and whose help he appreciates. At first, he worries that she may be spying on and gossiping about villagers and mildly disapproves. Later, "he felt it rather rude of Miss Menzies to refer to her new-found family of friends as 'creatures'" (*Aloft,* 44). Although he accompanies her to view their cottage, he seems inclined to "let live" (*Aloft,* 43). And he does. Miss Menzies is vastly different from Mr. Platter. Whereas he views the Borrowers as unknown creatures with economic value, she learns about their past and their race and knows their individual names. She respects their privacy and has come, as she tells Mr. Pott, to love them. Neither she nor her friend would ever think of exploiting them.

During the winter of the Clocks' imprisonment, both pairs of human beings are concerned with housing arrangements for the Borrowers. Mr. Platter plans and begins the building of a display house for his model village. Firmly encased in cement to prevent their burrowing out, it will have solid plate glass on one side and no place for the occupants to hide. "Can't have people asking for their money back," (*Aloft*, 103) he remarks. Pod realizes that, when the spring arrives, they will be in "a constant, unremitting state of being 'seen'" (*Aloft*, 104). By contrast, Mr. Pott and Miss Menzies, while examining the deserted house, notice how "bare it looked" (*Aloft*, 73) and spend the winter making it more comfortable for the occupants, should they ever return. He builds a working fire and lays in water and electricity; she constructs comfortable furniture and bedclothing.

Malevolent or benevolent as the intentions and actions of these people may be, they are ultimately detrimental to the well-being of the Clock family. Early in their stay at Vine Cottage, Pod and Homily enjoy a false sense of self-sufficiency, believing they are providing for themselves. Yet even though the renovations represent the fulfillment of Homily's wildest dreams, they rob Pod of the necessity of working himself and also increase the danger of their being seen and perhaps recaptured. Life as the principal attraction of the Platters' village would lead to their deaths. Both groups of human beings possess power over the Borrowers and thus rob them of the independence necessary for fulfilled lives. Unearned comfort and undeserved imprisonment are destructive. Arrietty, in renouncing human contact at the conclusion of the novel, has accepted a basic fact, not only of Borrower life but also of life in general.

In the presentation of this theme, Mary Norton is broadening the scope of the Borrowers series. No longer is the focus solely on the Clock family, its ingenious adaptation of human objects to its tiny world, or its hairbreadth escapes from homes that initially seemed secure. In fact, the plot seems somewhat mechanical and predictable, the account of the balloon's construction overly detailed and prolonged. The progress of Arrietty's course to maturity does possess symbolic depth, but her announcement that she will marry Spiller comes as no surprise to the reader. Pod and Homily are predictable in their reactions to the situations in which they find themselves. The human beings, all adults, with whom they interact are, however, given far greater attention than had been the case in the earlier books. The gentle, benevolent Mr. Pott; the lonely, sympathetic Miss Menzies; and the Platters, struggling fearfully but cruelly against their faltering economic situation, are as important characters as the Clocks and Spiller. Norton examines the motivations of people who have power over weaker, more vulnerable beings. With this shift of interest, the Clocks become vehicles in a plot designed to present a theme. And it is not a pleasant one. As Pod remarks, human beings are "never tamed. . . . One day, they'll break out—one day, when you least expect it" (*Aloft,* 184).

A Home at Last (Maybe): *The Borrowers Avenged*

What immediately strikes a reader of *The Borrowers Avenged* is its length—the American edition, at 298 pages, is nearly 50 percent longer than the first four books—and the shift in the title to a past participle—an indication of a completed action and possibly a suggestion that the series will come to an end. Reviewers have criticized many of the elements that contribute to this length—"an ungainly degree of contrivance," "inert, time-killing dialogue," and "minutiae" (Senick, 227) that overwhelm the reader. Indeed, the plot itself is abandoned for many chapters, particularly those describing the Clocks' trip from the river to the rectory, the explorations of the various nooks and crannies of the rectory, and the renovations to their new home. Nonetheless, it has a unity and provides a fitting conclusion to the series. In terms of the plot, the Platters will no longer be a menace to the Clocks; because Arrietty, for the first time in the series, has refrained from talking to a human being and has not been seen by one, the Clocks' dwelling place is unlikely to be discovered. In many ways, it is like Firbank Hall, but with advantages that place did not possess.

Yet a major question must be answered. Why, after two decades, did Mary Norton return to a series she had apparently completed with the publication of *The Borrowers Aloft?* In the epilogue to that book, the narrator hypothesized about the futures of the characters and remarked, "[Y]our [the reader's] guess will be just as true as mine" (*Aloft,* 192). Even so, just as *The Borrowers Afield* showed that neither Mrs. May's nor Kate's guesses in *The Borrowers* about what happened to the Clocks were correct, *The Borrowers Avenged* shows that more happened to the Clocks than the narrator guessed. In a sense, the narrator of *The Borrowers Aloft* is in a parallel situation to that of Jack-the-Giant-Killer, who, in *Are All the Giants Dead?,* has been acting for years as if all the giants were dead. She has been acting for many years as if the story were over, while, she may have known it was not. Imperfect though it may be in the telling, *The Borrowers Avenged* completes the story, providing on many levels as much closure as is possible. Most significant is the completion of the Clocks' search for a secure home and Arrietty's growth to maturity. In many ways, *The Borrowers Avenged* does for the Borrowers series what *The Stones of Green Knowe* did for Lucy M. Boston's Green Knowe series. That book, also written many years after the earlier volumes in its series, closed the saga.

The Clocks' adventures began because the home at Firbank was becoming inadequate. Arrietty, at the edge of adolescence, was restive in her confined environment; the family had become too dependent on the boy's borrowings; and, having been seen, they were in mortal danger if they remained. Moreover, there were no other Borrowers around, no friends for Arrietty, no prospective mates. The danger of their becoming extinct was a real possibility. Subsequent homes proved inadequate. The boot and kettle were too close to nature, too easily moved, and too easily seen by human beings. The interwall apartment at the gamekeeper's cottage was high above ground, too close to the Hendreary family (for Homily), not sufficiently accessible to the outdoors (for Arrietty), possessed of inadequate borrowing opportunities (for Pod), and, with the departure of Tom Goodenough and his uncle, devoid of human beings on whose presence successful borrowing depended. The security of Vine Cottage at Little Fordham is illusory. Early in *The Borrowers Avenged,* as the Clocks prepare once again to move, Arrietty thinks about the place: "Was it really home? . . . More of a hideaway, perhaps, after that long, dark winter in the Platters' attic" (*Avenged,* 33). Clearly, they need a place that offers them the security Firbank once did and the possibility of individual fulfillment and contentment for each of them.

When the Clock family enters the Old Rectory, Pod announces, "[W]e're home" (*Avenged,* 78). Gradually, the members of the family will each realize this place is even better than their first home. There are many similarities between the two residences: both are on the ground floor of large houses that contain very few human beings; both have gratings to the outside; and both offer ready access to large clocks (even the parts of a grandfather clock, in the rectory's game larder), books, and human food. Moreover, their new home has advantages not found in Firbank Hall. Their rooms are larger and brighter; the Clocks will live in a part of the house seldom entered by the human occupants, unlike the situation at Firbank, where they lived right under Mrs. Driver's kitchen; the grating is not cemented closed, but opens to the outdoors, leading to a fish pond, vines, and a vegetable garden; they have easy access to the library (for Arrietty), the larder (for Homily), and the junk-filled game larder (for Pod). The human beings are a happily married cook-house-keeper and gardener, very dissimilar to the power-seeking Driver and the cynical Crampfurl. The couple seldom venture beyond their quarters, and their presence or absence can be detected by noticing whether or not they answer the telephone. The wife, an Irishwoman, believes in fairies, so that even should she see the Clocks, she will accept them as supernatural beings. The Old Rectory also has two ghosts, the presence of whom seems to have driven most human occupants away. The house thus possesses the right balance of human presence and absence for Borrower well-being. The Old Rectory and the adjacent church contain other Borrowers. Here Arrietty meets Peagreen, an Overmantel who becomes her first nonhuman confidant and an "idea man" helpful to Pod as he renovates the apartment. The Hendrearys, living in the church, are nearby but not too close, and Spiller comes and goes.

After the Clocks' arrival, a third golden age of borrowing begins. The first, initiated by the boy, and the second, by Miss Menzies, were in fact not times of borrowing but times of receiving gifts. Nor, as the outcomes revealed, were they golden. Now they can borrow on a scale and range as never before. Each member of the family achieves fulfillment as a result of the freedom to borrow. Pod's "inventiveness knew no bounds. He had his old tools and he constructed others . . . [from] the jumble in the old game larder" (*Avenged,* 180); Homily happily cooks "splendid meals in her snow-white kitchen" (*Avenged,* 214); and Arrietty "was allowed to borrow, and not only that but, joy of joys, to borrow out of doors" (*Avenged,* 213). Peagreen rightly wonders, at the end of the novel, whether Borrowers are ever really safe. Yet at the Old Rectory, the Clocks have found the greatest security and contentment they have known since before Pod was seen by the boy at Firbank Hall.

The nature of the security and contentment achieved by Pod and Homily, and the harmony of their relationship, can be more fully understood by comparing them with the Hendrearys and the Platters. As they had been years ago, the Clocks and the Hendrearys are again neighbors. Each family had emigrated from Firbank Hall because the husband had been seen while on a borrowing expedition undertaken to please his wife. Both couples and their families had been afield, had been evicted from temporary lodgings (the Hendrearys from the badger set by foxes and the Clocks from their boot because of Mild Eye's rediscovery of it), had been forced to emigrate from the gamekeeper's cottage after Tom's departure, and, with Spiller's help, had relocated in the church and its rectory.

Nonetheless, their travels and destinations, as well as their situations at the end of *The Borrowers Avenged,* are very different. Although Aunt Lupy tells Homily that, like the Clocks, her family has had "some things that happened . . . that you'll hardly credit" (*Avenged,* 201), the fact is that they have had no adventures of the magnitude of those of Pod, Homily, and Arrietty. Having virtually driven the Clocks from the game-keeper's cottage, they have been led by Spiller to the church. There, although amply supplied with candle ends, they depend for food on dis-cards from the twice-weekly visits of Lady Mullings and Miss Menzies and the leavings of Kitty Whitlace's "elevenses." By Aunt Lupy's own admission, gathering food is difficult. Uncle Hendreary is becoming, as Pod remarks, "a martyr to gout" (*Avenged,* 276) and cannot easily borrow from the Whitlace's vegetable garden, while Timmus is too young to go out on his own. In addition, they are extremely close to human beings and in danger of being seen. When the church is filled with people, they must sit in darkness in their home inside an abandoned harmonium. At the end of the story, with Timmus having been seen, if only by the Platters, their security is far from certain.

The Platters, like the Hendrearys and the Clocks, have fallen on hard times. His kidnapping—not borrowing—and attempted recapture of the Clocks for display at his village is motivated not only as a means of overcoming these hard times but also because, as he tells his wife, "[w]e had a fortune in our hands" (*Avenged,* 28). A craftsman, as Pod is, Mr. Platter has used his skills to build ugly, poorly constructed villas for workers; to make additions to his model village in haste; and now to perform odd jobs, one of them being to repair windows he had installed for Lady Mullings only a few months earlier. Unlike Pod, who lovingly constructs Homily's kitchen in their new home, he would tear his own house down, brick by brick, to find the Borrowers, oblivious of his wife's entreaties: "It's the nicest house you ever built. . . . It's our *home,* Sidney" (*Avenged,* 28). His finest handiwork in his own eyes is "that showcase I made for *them*" (*Avenged,* 28), the glass-walled model house designed to be a prison, not a home for the Borrowers, a display area that will make his fortune.

The Clocks' happiness as they create a new home together, as opposed to the tenuousness of the Hendrearys' life and the shame and ruin of the Platters', may be as much a result of the nature of their relationships as it is of any physical circumstances. Never very charitable, and in Lupy's case snobbish, the Hendrearys complain of old age and show little evi-dence of being mutually supportive. Mr. Platter is mean-spirited, oblivi-ous to his wife's earnest and often tender concern for him. By contrast, Pod and Homily have worked together throughout their adventures. Given his conservatism and her squeamishness and reverse snobbery, each is proud of the other, offering moral and physical support. Pod borrows, often at considerable risk, to provide them with a good home, while Homily maintains a good home for him to return to after his expeditions.

The relationships between these pairs of adults can be used as a background against which to measure the final phase of Arrietty's growth to adulthood, an adulthood in which, as Norton reported in the epilogue to *The Borrowers Aloft,* she "will marry Spiller of course . . . , and they will have a fine, adventurous life—far freer than that of her parents" (*Aloft,* 192). The closure of her bildungsroman will be reached when she is able to form a mature relationship with her green-world lover. Since the beginning of *The Borrowers,* her meetings with human beings and experiences in nature had broken down her self-centered and ethnocentric perspectives. Her gradually increasing understanding of and admiration for Spiller had led her to the realization that she wishes to marry him.[9]

What more must happen to Arrietty before she will be ready for an adult relationship with Spiller? What she does not need, as is obvious from the plot, are further dangerous adventures. Although she sees the Platters on the departure from Little Fordham, she and her family are not seen and make their way to the Old Rectory with little difficulty. Arrietty is nearly seen twice by Kitty Whitlace, but these are presented as minor incidents and quickly passed over by the narrator. She is in no danger during the climactic scene in the church, observing Timmus and the Platters from the safety of an overlooking ledge. The important occurrences for Arrietty in *The Borrowers Avenged* are quieter and frequently more inward. At her new home, she experiences a greater feeling of both independence and interdependence. Her fuller sense of herself as an individual and a member of both her family and the Borrower race leads to her realization, in the final chapter, of the nature of her relationship with Spiller.

As the family prepares to leave Little Fordham, she is as ambivalent about it as she had been about Firbank Hall: "We were all right here, . . . before those Platters stole us. All the same, it lacked something—it was perhaps too ordered, too perfect, and in some way too confined. Improvisation is the breath of life to borrowers, and here was nothing they had striven for, planned, borrowed, or invented" (*Avenged,* 33). A new depth appears in her ambivalence here, for she thinks not just of herself but of her family as Borrowers. During the time she and Homily await Pod's return, she is in control of the situation: warning her mother of dangers, forbidding the use of lights or a fire, and offering comfort, as she also does on the boat trip upriver. Along the way, Arrietty has a

sense of freedom and exhilaration: "spring was just around the corner. . . .
And a new life" (*Avenged,* 62). The sight of vines on the rectory walls
excites her; she is pleased that the abundance of cover will permit ample
outdoor exploring and borrowing: "Suddenly she realized that she loved
this house, the garden, the sense of freedom, and she felt that somehow,
by some means yet to be discovered, they would find happiness here"
(*Avenged,* 108–9). Although momentarily dismayed when she thinks that
their apartments look like their confining home beneath the floorboards
of Mrs. Driver's kitchen, Arrietty is delighted to discover a grating like
the old one, but one "[y]ou could walk out on . . . into the sunlit world
outside" (*Avenged,* 132). Arrietty later considers that spring "one of the
happiest periods of her life" (*Avenged,* 180). Contributing as an adult to
the well-being of the family, she is allowed to borrow, as she had long
wished, and given the freedom to do so outdoors and to be innovative in
her methods. She has achieved the type of home life she had dreamed of
at Firbank.[10]

Arrietty spends much of her time wondering about and realizing the
significance of events and other people. In fact, forms of the words *wonder* and *realize* are frequently used in reference to her thoughts and
insights, which reveal her becoming more sensitive to other people and
more aware of herself. She wonders why so much happens to her family
in May, why her excitement about departing from Little Fordham is
tinged with sadness at leaving Miss Menzies, and what kind of new life
awaits them. She realizes that she could not kill a living creature, that
she has benefited as much from her companionship with Timmus as he
had, that she had liked Firbank "only because she had known no other
life" (*Avenged,* 126), and that she is going to like the Old Rectory.

More important, she has perceptions about other people that form
part of her growing sympathy for and understanding of them. Whereas
her initial meeting with the boy had been marked by extreme self-centeredness, she now perceives others' actions and beliefs from their point of
view. When she first meets Peagreen, for example, "she realized [that his
heart] . . . must be beating as hard as hers was" (*Avenged,* 92). She realizes
that Pod will not admonish his wife, because of his kindness, and looking
at the church, she "realized with what loving care Mr. Pott had copied the
original" (*Avenged,* 113). She understands Peagreen's reluctance to face
her parents after the near sighting by Kitty Whitlace in the kitchen and
knows that Mr. Platter reaches up to the rood screen because he "had
only been trying to humor Mrs. Platter" (*Avenged,* 266). Arrietty also
shows greater awareness of and admiration for her parents. On the eve of

the departure from Little Fordham, she is patient with Homily: "She knew her mother in this mood. After all, Homily had been brave enough in their other escapes . . . . A worrier she might be, but she would always rise to an emergency" (*Avenged*, 34–35). And she "had foreseen [that] the jumble on the old game larder [would provide Pod] with an almost endless supply of wonderful odds and ends" (*Avenged*, 180).

This sensitivity to others and the extent of Arrietty's maturation are seen in her encounter with the ghosts of the Old Rectory, an episode that at first glance might seem to be unnecessary padding in an already overlong novel. When she first sees the ghost of the young man "who had somehow got himself shot" (*Avenged*, 186), she initially feels pity, and she is annoyed because she thinks Pod and Peagreen's walking through him is a sign of disrespect. She is able to accept the reality of what the young man and girl now are, harmless, incorporeal beings, and of what they once were, unhappy human beings. Still, as Homily had earlier said, "ghosts is too self-centered to take a blind bit of notice of human beans" (*Avenged*, 44), or, for that matter, of Borrowers. Indeed, the ones at the Old Rectory are self-centered, the little girl nourishing through eternity her grief for the young man who (it is strongly implied) committed suicide. They may well symbolize the dangers of self-absorption, and in putting thoughts of them behind her, Arrietty reveals the extent of her movement away from childish self-centeredness.

Arrietty also comes to a much fuller understanding and acceptance of the rules that govern the lives of Borrowers, particularly the prohibition of making contacts with human beings, about which Pod had warned her in the final chapter of *The Borrowers Aloft*. *The Borrowers Avenged* details the considerable struggle she undergoes in keeping her promise not to speak to Miss Menzies, and in doing so, Arrietty accepts her status as an adult Borrower, one who puts the safety of her family, friends, and ultimately her race ahead of personal wishes or inclinations. Her promise has been made at great personal sacrifice. Of the three human beings with whom she has spoken, Arrietty has the deepest feelings for Miss Menzies, from whom she learned a great deal about adult male-female relationships and their failures. Because she understands Miss Menzies's sensitivity and kindness toward others, she wishes to allay the anxiety and grief she knows her friend must be suffering over the Clocks' disappearance. Her one regret at leaving Little Fordham is her realization that in Miss Menzies, she "knew she was losing a friend" (*Avenged*, 47). When she learns that the woman is a frequent visitor to the church, she unsuccessfully pleads with Homily to be allowed to "speak to her just *once!*" (*Avenged,* 227) and is unhappy, the Saturday before Easter, because she fears she will not see the woman, even though she is so near to her. When, however, Arrietty does view her during the climactic events that night, she remembers her promise despite the fact that, as she tells Spiller, "[s]ometimes I was close enough to speak to her" (*Avenged,* 294).

Significantly, as she views the events in the church, "Arrietty realized the utter helplessness of their tiny race when pitted against human odds" (*Avenged,* 276), and although she looks longingly at Miss Menzies, her greatest concern is not for her friend: "Dear Miss Menzies, thought Arrietty, protector of everyone, but, all the same, she wished they would go. She was longing to see Timmus" (*Avenged,* 292). Not only is her concern for the safety of a fellow Borrower greater than her wish to communicate with a beloved human being but also motherly instincts, which have been developing through the novel, are dominant. When she first hears of the Hendrearys' residence at the church, she immediately says, "I'd love to see Timmus" (*Avenged,* 39). Gazing at the church shortly after the arrival, she realizes how much she loves him, remembers Aunt Lupy's patronizing remark about her being a little mother, and thinks, "Yes, perhaps she had been a 'little mother' to Timmus; perhaps she had made his dull, young life a little less dull" (*Avenged,* 114). After their reunion, she takes charge of him, teaching him about borrowing out of doors, worrying about his wild escapades, correcting his grammar, and telling him stories. Hers are the reactions of a maturing individual, one for whom marriage and motherhood may not be far away.

Before marriage, however, Arrietty's relationship with Spiller must undergo further development, much of which occurs in connection with her new friendship with Peagreen, the lame young Overmantel who has resided in the Old Rectory all his life. Kuznets makes the observation that "whether Peagreen will become Spiller's rival for Arrietty's hand . . . is left open for the reader's guessing" (Kuznets 1985b, 76). Yet this seems unlikely. While he and Arrietty share a love of reading and climbing, he does not like the outdoors, partly because of his lameness; is not good with his hands (although he has many good ideas about interior decoration, which both Pod and Homily appreciate); and enjoys his solitary life in his new bachelor quarters. Not only is his personality very different from Arrietty's, but also she never shows the kind of interest in him that she does in Spiller. In fact, at times, she exhibits a kind of motherly pity for his lameness. Peagreen is a good friend, a confidant, and the first nonhuman adult friend she has had. As such, he is able to help her better understand Spiller and her attitudes toward him. As her first Borrower friend, he is an indication of the extent to which she is weaning herself from the compulsion to befriend human beings. But he is a direct contrast to Spiller in his artistic ability, his upper-class background, his physical limitations, and his cleanliness. Finally, he is less careful than Spiller, taking Arrietty dangerously across the open kitchen floor, nearly causing them to be seen, something Spiller would never do. Although both are loners, Spiller, not Peagreen, is the man for Arrietty.

Spiller plays a small role in *The Borrowers Avenged.* He takes the Clocks from Little Fordham to the Old Rectory, borrows food for them from the larder, keeps the field mice down in the garden, and catches an occasional minnow for their supper. He speaks only twice in the novel, remarking that human beings sometimes talk truthfully into the telephone and, later, explaining that he had brought the Clocks' belongings to the edge of the pond because he knew they'd be moving in. He says nothing in the final scene, during which he and Peagreen hear Arrietty's account of the events in the church. During the novel, his character is unchanged and he exhibits the silence, intuitive understanding, and reliability he had shown in the previous books.

What does change is Arrietty's understanding of him. During the family's escape upriver, her attitude toward him is one of admiration and gratitude: "Oh, blessed Spiller! Oh, blessed, silent knitting needle, driving them swiftly forwards in Spiller's nimble hands" (*Avenged,* 60). Her thoughts seem to be less on the escape than on Spiller's role in it. After the landing, "Arrietty looked round for Spiller, but she could not see him. This was nothing new: he could melt into any background provided (this she remembered) that background was out of doors" (*Avenged,* 70). This event may be symbolic of Arrietty's lack of perception, at this point, of Spiller as an individual. She does not see or understand him to any great degree. She enjoys the outdoor activities they share, and at the end of *The Borrowers Aloft,* had unilaterally decided but did not communicate to him her decision to marry him. She does not really consider him on his own terms; rather, she sees him only as he relates to her needs, wants, and inclinations. If she is to achieve a mature relationship with him, she must be able figuratively to place him in the foreground, to distinguish him from the background into which he can blend, not only because of his solitariness and shyness but also because of her failure to perceive his character.

The first step occurs during their trek from the riverbank to the rectory. As they pause to rest, Arrietty notices Spiller stretched out on the ground: "Odd that she had never thought of Spiller as one who could be tired, or even as one who slept. . . . How kind Spiller had always been to them! And yet, in a way, so distant: one could never talk to Spiller except about the barest essentials. Oh, well, she supposed one could not have everything" (*Avenged,* 71). With her increasing awareness, Arrietty begins to wonder and perhaps to worry about a future with him: "Would he come to live in this house with them? . . . Helping them to borrow and perhaps taking Pod's place when Pod got older? . . . The answer . . . was no: Spiller, that outdoor creature, would never live in a house, never throw his lot in with theirs. But he would help them, always help them—of that she was sure" (*Avenged,* 90). Hers are assumptions, and in making them, she ignores the facts that Spiller had visited the house and explored it thoroughly before bringing her family to it and has borrowed food from the larder for them at least twice. For them, especially for her, he does come into the house. Later, when Spiller indicates that he knew they'd stay at the rectory, Arrietty comprehends that "with his sharp, wild instincts, [he] understood them better than they understood themselves" (*Avenged,* 164–65). He certainly understands them better than Arrietty understands him, although she is learning.

Arrietty's major insight into Spiller's character and her relationship with him occurs in the final chapter. As she narrates Saturday's events to Peagreen and Spiller, the latter pauses in his errand and "condescended to squat on his haunches . . . to hear it to the end. His eyes looked very bright, but he did not speak a word" (*Avenged,* 294). Though he is intensely interested in her welfare, she seems not to notice, and in her self-centeredness she tells how, against her wishes, she did not speak to Miss Menzies. Angrily she turns on him: "'You once said *you'd* tell her,' she accused him, 'that we were safe and all that. But I knew you wouldn't. You're much too scared of human beans—even lovely ones like Miss Menzies. Let alone *speak* to one!'" (*Avenged,* 295). After Spiller's abrupt departure, "Arrietty said in a surprised voice, 'He's angry'" (*Avenged,* 295). Peagreen's remark that it is not surprising challenges her assertion that she spoke the truth and makes her realize that she has been wrong in her judgment of Spiller. Had she got past her self-pity, she would have remembered his friendship with Tom Goodenough and his bravery against Mild Eye. She would also have realized that just as she had kept her promise to Pod, so too would he, as Homily had assured her at Vine Cottage, keep his to her. But she would also have understood, as Peagreen explains, that "he's a law unto himself, . . . he'll choose his own moment" (*Avenged,* 296). Peagreen helps her to see her own fault and to realize that she should have trusted Spiller. Trust must be the basis of their relationship.

Having come to a fuller understanding of herself and Spiller, she simply states to Peagreen, "You see, really, I do rather like him" (*Avenged,* 297). Given the times and the fact that Peagreen is somewhat proper and not a family member, Arrietty's understated remark is essentially a public declaration of her love for Spiller. With Peagreen's assurance that "he'll get over it" (*Avenged,* 296), their reconciliation seems almost certain. Arrietty has now left her childhood, has traveled through her uncertain adolescence, and is ready for an adult love relationship with Spiller.

One final aspect of *The Borrowers Avenged* needs to be considered, as it contributes to the effect of closure achieved by the novel: the large amount of satire of early twentieth-century life.[11] While in its quantity it may appear gratuitous, the presentation of some of the author's own pet peeves, it is functional, a commentary on the larger worlds the Clocks must concern themselves with in their continual quest for survival and security. In the earlier books, there had been generalized satire of human nature in the description of characters and actions of both Borrowers and human beings; however, individuals, not social forces, had been examined and had been the threats to the Clocks at Firbank and Tom Goodenough's cottage. The older ways of English country life represented few threats to cautious, cooperative Borrowers. Even Mild Eye, who had considered exhibiting the tiny people for pennies, was a product of earlier times and relatively easily discouraged in his search for them.

With the move to Little Fordham and then into the village, though, the Clocks are coming into closer contact with life of the twentieth century. Modern life is at best unaesthetic and artistically tasteless. Peagreen laments the enthusiasm for art nouveau of the most recent human tenants of the Old Rectory. They had "spoiled the look" (*Avenged,* 99) of the library, as even Arrietty notices, tearing down the overmantel, blocking up the old fireplace, and installing a small grate. Laborers no longer live in cottages like that of Tom Goodenough, but in council houses, no doubt virtually identical, hastily and poorly built by people like Mr. Platter. Yet modernization has had devastating effects as well, as Arrietty realizes, considering the renovation of the library: "the overmantel gone, a whole life style destroyed" (*Avenged,* 96). In Mr. Platter's case, living in the modern world means making money with little concern for people's lives. Even observing people's deaths is no longer a meaningful ritual for him, but quite simply a business undertaking. This is also true for his riverside teas and model village. Unlike the true craftsman Mr. Pott, who uses donations to help others, money is an end for Platter. Mr. Pott himself is a victim of modern technology, having lost his leg in a railway accident.

Interestingly, the Borrowers have difficulty in understanding the concepts of money and banking. They, like Mr. Pott and to an extent Tom Goodenough and the church ladies, represent simpler, more traditional life-styles and values. Although they now live in closer proximity to more people than ever before, the Clocks' choice of the abandoned part of the Old Rectory and their avoidance of all contact with human beings indicate their withdrawal from the modern world and its evils. By presenting these evils in the extended satire, the narrator is able to indicate clearly that the Clocks' future happiness and security will be greater to the extent that they can escape these.

Narrative Voice, Point of View, Belief, and Maturity

As the summaries of the plots of the four Borrowers sequels indicated, each began with interactions between human beings. In *The Borrowers Afield* and *The Borrowers Afloat,* Kate engages in activities and conversations that offer explanations of how the events of the central narrative come to be told in the present. In *The Borrowers Aloft* and *The Borrowers Avenged,* the narrative frames are dropped and the focus is on adult human beings who interact with the Clock family. The last two books include brief postscripts in which a third-person narrator writes of the subsequent lives of the characters.

The dropping of the frame narratives including Kate and Mrs. May after *The Borrowers Afloat* has been noticed by some critics but, with one exception, has received scant critical attention. Kuznets has argued that the changes "are connected with a deepening commitment on Mary Norton's part to the notion of making her Borrower characters independent of all human beings" (Kuznets 1985b, 67). Just as the story of the Clocks' adventures is presented with successively fewer human intermediaries, so too do the Borrowers themselves come to depend less on human beings. Their downfall and rescue in *The Borrowers* are dependent on the boy and their rescue in *The Borrowers Afield* on Tom. While they think they are self-reliant during their early stay at Little Fordham, they are, with the exception of Arrietty, unwitting recipients of Miss Menzies's kindness. Their escape from the Platters' attic is the first they have engineered on their own, while in the final book, they are not seen and achieve as great a degree of independence from human beings as is possible given the nature of their lives.

In *The Borrowers,* the existence of the memory of the Clocks is entirely dependent on the interactions of Kate and Mrs. May. *The Borrowers Afield* is dependent on Kate. As Arrietty says hello to Tom Goodenough, readers know that she will tell Tom about the events that, in the opening narrative frame, he tells Kate. Such is not the case with *The Borrowers Afloat.* Tom would certainly have known about the Clocks' life until he left the gamekeeper's cottage with his uncle and would have told Kate about it. It is, however, highly unlikely that he would have learned of their later adventures from the shy, reticent, silent Spiller. While the transition between frame and central narratives in *The Borrowers* and *The Borrowers Afield* clearly indicates that the stories are the tellings of a person from the frame, such is not the case here. When Kate shows Mrs. May the Gothic-shaped hole, the old woman speculates on Homily's emotions as she enters her new home. Even so, the direct narrative begins, "But Mrs. May was not quite right" (*Afloat,* 24). What follows is unmediated narrative, independent of the suppositions of Kate and Mrs. May. This, as Kuznets notes (Kuznets 1985b, 1974), would explain the inclusion of the scene in which Mrs. Driver sat in the kitchen at Firbank. None of the human beings involved in the transmission of the narrative could have access to this scene. The narrative has achieved virtually independent status, as the Clocks will over the next two books.

The disappearance of the narrative frames parallels a major theme of the series: the growth to maturity of Arrietty as she acquires a greater sense of independence, breaks herself of the need for human contact, and realizes the value of interdependence in her Borrower family and community. The telling of the story of the Clock family's emigrations and odyssey had first required the narrative of Mrs. May, an adult, and then required her guidance of Kate. Kate, the child, nearly a year older, had befriended Tom on her own, and later, as an adult, had re-created the story he had told her. In subsequent volumes, the story exists on its own, without adult mediation. It is almost as if readers, like Arrietty, need successively less adult guidance to understand the lives presented. In the last two volumes, they are invited to confront, react to, and understand the narrative directly, as Arrietty must do with her world. In fact, readers are now capable of creating their own sequels, as the narrator suggests at the end of *The Borrowers Aloft:* "The story still goes on; but it is your turn now to tell it" (*Aloft,* 192).

Finally, the dropping of the frame narratives in the last two books relates to the theme of belief in the existence of the Borrowers. In the opening two books, Mrs. May assists Kate in achieving belief in events and characters. In *The Borrowers Afield,* Kate acquires facts—a visit to the scenes of the Clocks' adventures, confirmation of the existence of the human beings who had played parts in the original story, a meeting with a person who claimed to have met a Borrower, and possession of an object belonging to one of them—and follows Mrs. May's advice about sifting the evidence to solidify her belief in their existence. If Kate is the "author" of the last three books in the story, it is significant that virtually none of their contents are based on details supplied by encouraging adults. They quite likely contain Kate's own surmises and guesses. Nevertheless, telling the story without hard facts is acceptable; as Mrs. May, implying that absence of fact does not invalidate belief, tells Kate, "Anything we haven't experienced for ourselves sounds like a story" (*Afield,* 8). The continuing story of the Clock family can be told on the basis of belief rather than fact. The final two books do not need a framework. Like Kate, who has gone beyond the need for adult guidance, young readers can interact and accept the unmediated story, believing without the aid of framework and fact. Like the human beings in the adventures, their sympathetic belief is the key to imaginative response to the experiences and characters of the Borrowers: "So there you were, Kate decided—thinking it over afterwards—you could take it or leave it" (*Afield,* 4). Kate, in the end, took it. It is a tribute to Mary Norton's sustained artistry that most readers of the Clocks' odyssey, as she wrote it over nearly three decades, have taken it as well.

Chapter Five
Achieving Closure

Are All the Giants Dead?

Unlike *The Magic Bed-Knob* and *The Borrowers,* the foundations on which sequels—leading to closure—were erected, *Are All the Giants Dead?* does not belong to a series. Nonetheless, it could be considered a sequel to a hypothetical book by Mary Norton and to stories written by others. Whereas in *The Magic Bed-Knob,* the Wilson children meet Miss Price for the first time, and in *The Borrowers,* Arrietty establishes her first relationship with a human being, the boy, in the first paragraph of *Are All the Giants Dead?* James, the central character, thinks back on an earlier relationship: "she must be here again, that lady."[1] He seems to refer to the person who had evidently taken him on previous night journeys to visit "those 'old fairy-tale people'" (*Giants,* 16). Moreover, the fairy-tale people he meets are living in the period after the conclusion of the stories that have made them famous; this novel, then, is a sequel about their lives in the seldom examined "happily-ever-after" era. Because the title's question, *Are All the Giants Dead?* taken from an old poem, allows for a negative answer, the possibility arises that the conventional happily-ever-after closure of the old fairy tales is not as complete, as final, as is generally assumed. Thus, this novel is about true closure, the full resolution of conflicts. In the novel, James, an ordinary boy, plays an important role in events that lead to the fulfillment of the lives of Dulcibel, the princess who must marry a toad; Jack-of-the-Beanstalk; and Jack-the-Giant-Killer. It also brings a conclusion to James's nighttime trips with "that lady," Mildred, for his experiences on this journey help him to mature so much that he will not need to travel with her again. Like the boy in *The Borrowers,* he has been so changed as a result of his relationship with an unusual girl, Dulcibel, that he can move onward to the next stage of his development.

Life in the Happily-Ever-After: Narrative Variations on a Theme

The narrative begins as James awakens in the night to discover Mildred, a slender, slightly graying, middle-aged woman, sitting by the window of his strangely altered bedroom. Disengaging himself from his body, he walks with her through the deserted streets of his modern neighborhood toward a castle rising from "what . . . should have been the site of the Royal Hospital" (*Giants,* 16). While Mildred talks to three middle-aged women—Beauty, Sleeping Beauty, and Cinderella—James strikes up a conversation with Dulcibel, a princess playing near a well, and learns about the curse she is under: should her golden ball fall into the well, she must marry the resident toad. James reluctantly leaves her and accompanies Mildred through a postern gate into the forest toward her next destination, the town of Much-Belungun-under-Bluff. Shy and uncomfortable in the palace, he relaxes in the woods. Because he does not accept Mildred's belief that the toad will turn into a prince, he searches for a female toad as a mate for it. Mildred and James stop at an inn run by the famous Jacks, each of whom is upset when the other recounts his adventures to James. Jack-the-Giant-Killer is also annoyed by a set of dancing shoes that keep entering the inn. After Mildred leaves to report on a royal wedding, remarking as she departs that she had forgotten to lock the castle's postern gate, Jack-of-the-Beanstalk shows James the bluff, in which the boy is interested. That night, although Jack-the-Giant-Killer tells James about killing 12 giants, he refuses to speak of the thirteenth, whom he supposedly killed as well.

The next morning, exploring on his own for the first time during one of these trips, James follows the dancing shoes into the forest, where he sees Dulcibel, who informs him that the golden ball has fallen into the well and that a voice has announced that unless she marries the toad in seven days she, her parents, and the castle will vanish. Her only hope is to find a toad with a jewel in its head, with which, she thinks, the toad she must marry is in love. When James agrees to help her, the two travel to the home of Hecubenna, an aging, powerless witch, to seek advice. Her power had waned when, on a trip to the giant's bluff, she lost the jeweled toad, which protects its possessor. James learns that the thirteenth giant is still alive; that with the toad, he is immune to Jack-the-Giant-Killer's attacks; and that a crevice leads to the bluff top. Returning to the inn with Dulcibel, he explains the reasons for the old man's lack of success. Greatly relieved, Jack-the-Giant-Killer flings the thirteenth tress, really horsehair, into the fire, admitting the truth.

Late the next day, after James and Dulcibel have climbed the crevice to the bluff, a rainstorm forces them to seek shelter for the night. In the morning, James spots the giant searching for the protecting toad, which has escaped during the storm. When it leaps into Dulcibel's lap, the boy seizes it, and the two rush to escape the giant, who appears to stumble and fall. Jack-the-Giant-Killer has slain it, having climbed up a stalk that has grown from a bean his companion planted two nights before. James gives the toad to Dulcibel, to keep her from harm.

At this point, the adventure might well be over. As Norton remarks about the two Jacks, "The story for them had ended" (*Giants,* 116). Dulcibel, in possession of the protective toad, can return to the castle with no fear of anything bad happening to her. Little seems to need to be done but to reunite James with Mildred and return him to his own bedroom. But as Mrs. May said to Kate in *The Borrowers,* much more happens. After Dulcibel has left for her home, James notices the magical toad on the other side of the stream. Apparently unknown to the princess, it has escaped, and she is riding into her future unprotected. James returns sadly to the inn, falls into a troubled sleep, and awakens to find that Mildred is back. She had heard of Dulcibel's problem and rushed to the castle, where she learned that the princess had gone straight to the well and proposed to the toad. The result had not been what James had expected: a handsome young prince emerged and accepted her proposal. Dulcibel had known she was without magic protection and had bravely confronted her future. Lying in bed, thinking about events, James hears the slam of a car door, realizes he is back in his own room, falls asleep, and begins to dream about cosmonauts.

This plot outline reveals general similarities between *Are All the Giants Dead?* and Norton's earlier books. It involves an ordinary child on a circular journey, leaving home for a new, different, and wonderful territory; making important friendships; and then returning. The Wilson children moved from London, to their Aunt Beatrice's, to Miss Price's, to other times and places, and back to London. In *The Borrowers,* Mrs. May's brother traveled from his family home in India, to Firbank Hall, to the edge of the Clock family's home, and back to India. Kate, with the help of Mrs. May, traveled imaginatively from the breakfast room, to the long-ago time and place of Arrietty's world, and back to the present. In addition, the central young human being in each of these novels established an important relationship with an adult who is in some ways a mentor—Carey with Miss Price and Kate with Mrs. May—and with individuals from different worlds—the Wilsons with Emelius Jones and the boy and Tom Goodenough with Arrietty. As is the case with Arrietty and the boy, the relationships influence the individual from the different world.

Despite the similarities to Norton's previous works, *Are All the Giants Dead?* is not a simple reworking of themes, plot patterns, and character groupings. Major authors do, of course, focus on certain themes, but they return to them from different angles, examining heretofore unresolved or undiscovered concerns. The achievement of *Are All the Giants Dead?* can be better appreciated by considering initially how the novel differs from its predecessors in its presentation of somewhat similar events and character types. In the first place, the circular journey takes the character to a completely fantastic, magical location. Miss Price had traveled with the Wilson children to unlikely but actual places, albeit by magical means, while the boy discovered Arrietty living beneath the floorboards of a typical country house in Bedfordshire. James, however, travels out of body to a place inhabited by characters who live only in stories, specifically folktales and literary fairy tales; he meets individuals who exist only through the agency of the literary imagination. Arrietty had been insulted when the boy said she was a fairy, retorting that she didn't believe in their existence; the boy had to accept her corporeal reality. This is not an issue for James. The destiny of the Clock family is strongly influenced by the activities of the boy; Dulcibel's happy marriage is not influenced by James.

Finally, the novel is written in a completely different genre from that of the other works: the dream journey. The events take place after James has first gone to sleep in his own bed and before he awakens back in it. Most children's dream journey stories, however, including Lewis Carroll's *Alice's Adventures in Wonderland,* Maurice Sendak's *Where the Wild Things Are,* and the Judy Garland movie version of *The Wizard of Oz,* take place specifically within the mind/imagination of the narrator. The paradigm of the story is usually as follows: the central characters, troubled by elements of the waking world, fall asleep and enter a world where they confront the troubling aspects in altered form. When they resolve the conflicts, they awaken better able to relate to the waking world.

This pattern, other than its circular movement to and from the waking world, is not seen in *Are All the Giants Dead?* James appears to have no problems in his life; it seems virtually impossible to reconstruct his waking life from elements in the night adventures (as it is, for example, in *Alice in Wonderland*); and he deals with no major inner anxieties and conflicts during the adventures. Perhaps the clue to the nature of the experience is to be found in the description of the beginning of James' journey: "'Where are we going?' he asked, as he disentangled his leg from his old leg. He no longer noticed the strange feeling this gave him—he was used now to walking about the room and still seeing himself lying there on the bed—a good imitation of himself, really, he thought" (*Giants,* 14). Norton seems to be presenting this as an out-of-body experience, not unlike that of African dreamers or Eskimo shamans, an actual journey to different realms of experience, different dimensions of being. As the shaman is able to make his trip partly through the agency of his tutelary spirits, so James is able to make his trips, which appear to have occurred frequently, because of the power and through the assistance of Mildred.

If, then, James has made this kind of journey, rather than the conventional dream-inside-the-head journey, an important question arises. Why did this boy make this specific out-of-body trip, encountering and interacting with these specific characters, assisted by this woman, Mildred? In seeking an answer to this question, we may come closer to understanding the meanings of the novel and appreciating the originality and artistry of its presentation.

James's Long Night's Journey through the Land of Fairy Tales

Why James? In his waking life, he seems to be an average boy, interested in performing experiments with his chemistry set, enjoying stops with his parents at country pubs where he can have Coca-Cola and potato chips and can depend on the adults becoming "suddenly inclined to spoil" (*Giants,* 46) on the trip home, and looking forward to a new bicycle for his birthday. He enjoys science fiction, having little memory of the fairy tales he read long ago at his grandmother's house. In fact, as many of his reactions during the novel reveal, he is virtually ignorant of the famous characters and the conventions of these stories. He does not understand why spells must be in rhyme and does not realize that an object pinned to an old oak tree is a charm designed to keep witches away. Mildred has already taken James on several excursions to the land of fairy-tale characters, and he although admits that she has an ability to make "things that seemed strange at first, and somewhat false, gradually [become] quite real" (*Giants,* 40), and that "sometimes these [excursions] could be interesting" (*Giants,* 16), he has little interest in the present journey: "He slowed his steps a little, guessing what they were in for: some of those 'old fairy-tale people' again" (*Giants,* 16). While James seems unlikely to be a hero in the adventures that follow, he may be just the individual who can most benefit from them. Average, bored, somewhat flippant, and ignorant of and uncaring about fairy tales, he needs experiences that will help him to grow and develop as an individual. While he is in many ways unlike the boy in *The Borrowers,* he too is about to enter a period of his life that will profoundly influence his character.

Until he talks with Dulcibel, James shows little interest in events, responding with a flat "Oh" (*Giants,* 25) when Mildred tells him they have just met famous fairy-tale characters, and he first dismisses Dulcibel as "the usual golden-haired girl, playing with the usual golden ball" (*Giants,* 16). But alone with her shortly thereafter, he responds to her account of the curse by staring "incredulously" (*Giants,* 30) and questioning her "in an unbelieving voice" (*Giants,* 30). He is impressed by her certainty about her situation and begins to perceive her loneliness, thinking, "perhaps she had never had a friend" (*Giants,* 32), and understanding that she offers to let him play with her cup and ball because "she was trying to keep them [James and Mildred]" (*Giants,* 32).

By the time James and Mildred have left the courtyard through the postern gate, he has learned about the female toad that might save Dulcibel from marriage to the toad and has had his first glimpse of the distant bluffs he later climbs. As he becomes more concerned about the princess's fate, both the toad and the bluff will become increasingly interrelated. Walking through the forest, James becomes interested as Mildred discusses the importance of the toad for Dulcibel, wanting to believe, but skeptically remarking, "[I]f I were Dulcibel, I wouldn't bank on it" (*Giants,* 41). Later, as he plays in a forest pond, he remembers the girl's remark and begins searching for the toad. Although Mildred warns him, "[O]ne must never become too involved in their lives: it always leads to trouble" (*Giants,* 42)—a remark reminiscent of Pod's words to Arrietty about relationships with human beings—James's fruitless quest marks a positive step in his character growth. No longer is he uninterested in the people he meets on these excursions; he genuinely wants to help another person. Incredulous earlier, a person, as Dulcibel recognized, "from some other country" (*Giants,* 32), he is now acting on the basis of knowledge he has acquired and is beginning to believe. As Mildred says of his actions, "[I]t was very kind and thought-

ful of you" (*Giants,* 43). After they have noticed Big Hans's charm mark-
ing the way to the home of the old witch Hecubenna, "James, lagging
behind, plucked a stalk of grass and began to chew it. He was thinking
of witches and of what Dulcibel had said. That path beside the oak tree
had looked well worn" (*Giants,* 44). He remembers that Dulcibel had
believed that the female toad was in the hands of a witch, and the well-
worn quality of the path suggests to him that the witch may still be
there. Thoughts of Dulcibel and her deliverance are still with him. He
does not share these with Mildred, however, thus making one step
toward his first independent actions.

When he meets the two Jacks, James is impressed. Instead of the flat
response he made at the castle, he gasps an "'Oh!' . . . He was amazed"
(*Giants,* 47). Mildred has finally introduced him to fairy-tale characters
who interest him. Not the courtly individuals who are the subjects of
Mildred's magazine articles, these old men are heroes to whom the boy
can relate, performers of daring physical deeds who live at the edge of a
forest James likes because "it was more a boy's kind of place" (*Giants,*
39). After looking at their "smiling, uncertain faces" (*Giants,* 52), he
chooses to stay with them instead of accompanying Mildred to the royal
wedding. This decision is a turning point in his development. He leaves
the safety of the woman who "knew the ropes" (*Giants,* 52) because he is
impressed by the two men and sensitive to their kindness and uncertainty. Still, Jack-the-Giant-Killer's refusal to talk about the encounter with
the thirteenth giant upsets him: "'Oh, do go on,' begged James. 'Just
tell me about this last one!'" (*Giants,* 59). His response is like Kate's to
Mrs. May late in *The Borrowers,* and like Kate, he will later take an active
role in completing the story. But his role is not purely imaginative as is
hers. James must himself find answers to the mystery of the bluff and
Jack's refusal to tell the entire story. Doing so, he will not only mature as
an individual, but he will help to create closure to the stories of Dulcibel
and the two Jacks.

Before his reunion with Dulcibel by the pond in the forest, several
small incidents subtly indicate how much James has changed since the
last time he was at this spot. At the inn, he appreciates the artistry of
Jack's cooking, his using brushwood "as delicately as a painter uses a
palette" (*Giants,* 61). Leaving the house intending to explore the crevice,
he wisely takes along a hawthorn stick, no doubt aware of the magical
power of that wood. He is sensitively aware of the dancing shoes, thinking that Jack-of-the-Beanstalk could be right in believing that they
might want to tell him something or lead him somewhere. Along the

way, he learns to adapt his pace to their erratic movements, stops to rescue a beetle from attacking ants, and, spotting a magpie, remembers the folksaying "One for sorrow, two for joy" (*Giants*, 63). Imperceptibly, perhaps unknown even to himself, James is accepting the folktale world into which he has ventured. He meets Dulcibel, with whom he will journey to the bluff in search of the toad, because he trusted the shoes. His small act of kindness to the beetle prefigures his later good deeds.

Although he still does not understand all of the characteristics of this new world, asking, for example, "Why do they [bad fairies] always talk in rhyme?" (*Giants*, 68), he quickly takes control of the situation, calming Dulcibel by telling her that they have an entire week to find a solution, offering to help her search for the magic toad, and suggesting that Hecubenna, the nearby witch, may have it. Frightened though he admits he is of witches, he urges the princess to follow him and to "try to be brave" (*Giants*, 71). He enters the witch's hut alone and decides "to tell [Hecubenna] everything: it was the only way, he realized, that they might get help" (*Giants*, 77). Having acquired knowledge of the toad's whereabouts and of a way to the top of the bluff, he now understands the cause of the two Jacks' melancholy. As Tabitha, the housekeeper, explains, "They think they're past it" (*Giants*, 78). He has received the information because he sensitively understands the woman's character: "Perhaps because of her lonely life, Miss Tabitha seemed happy to keep him by her and willing to tell him much" (*Giants*, 76).

The next morning, James awakens thinking, "Everything was turning out very sad, very difficult, very dangerous" (*Giants*, 86), and wishing that Mildred were there. Because there is nothing else to do, he suggests to Dulcibel that they look at the crevice. He helps her to overcome her fears about bats and realizes that he cannot proceed without her help. At the top, their sense of achievement is short-lived; new problems await them. Pinprickel, the evil fairy who had set the curse on Dulcibel, has discovered their whereabouts and is lurking in the crevice below; the crevice is sealed by a rainstorm; and the giant sees them. James has misgivings about the rightness of his helping Dulcibel by bringing her here: "[H]e remembered Mildred's warning him and saying that pleasant as it was to visit 'these people' that 'one must never become too involved in their lives,' that 'it always led to trouble' as indeed it had. But, he reminded himself, Dulcibel had come to him for help, and he had tried to help her" (*Giants*, 100). When they are noticed by the giant, James's quick action—scooping the magical toad into his hand, depriving the giant of its protection—makes it possible for Jack-the-Giant-Killer to slay his enemy. James directs the panicking Dulcibel to the only safe area on the bluff, an overhang that would be too weak to support the giant's weight. The danger over, he presents the toad to the princess, announcing, "Now nothing can ever harm you" (*Giants*, 108). James is not a giant-killer. In fact, Jack's killing of the giant turns out to have been very easy and not very dangerous at all. James's heroism is of a different kind. By keeping his head and using his wits, he comes up with the best solution possible for saving the life of a person whom he no longer considers just a typical fairy-tale girl. Finding the magical toad allows him to help the two Jacks complete their stories and perhaps provides Dulcibel with the means for completing hers. Moreover, he has acted without Mildred's assistance.

Whereas up to this point James has tried to assist Dulcibel, now he attempts to direct the course of her life, telling her to go directly to the well and propose to the toad, trusting to the protection of the second toad. Significantly, he uses the word *must* four times in his directions to her. Yet as she prepares to leave, he senses that "Dulcibel, on her great white charger, seemed very high and far away (in all senses of these words)" (*Giants*, 115–16). The princess, he later learns, has released the magic toad, preferring to face her future on her own. She appears to have been considering the action from the time she left the inn, but now, more mature and independent herself, has not told James. Instead, she let him make up a rhyme and praised him for it, keeping her own counsel.

James, though, is unaware of her decision, and when he sees the toad at the pond, he panics for the first time in the novel, dashing into the flood-swollen stream after it. On his return to the inn, he gives in to despair, weeping himself to sleep. Thoughtful of others' feelings, he allows the two Jacks to retain their newfound happiness by not reporting the toad's escape and thinks better of reminding Mildred about her failure to lock the postern gate, because "a reminder might upset her" (*Giants*, 120). But when he hears that Dulcibel has not used his rhyming lines and has proposed to the toad without her talisman, he "groaned. He put his hands to his brow and rocked slowly from side to side" (*Giants*, 121). In bed, James experiences an epiphany, a flash of understanding that marks his greatest step toward maturity in the novel: "Dulcibel had not needed a talisman; all she had needed was courage" (*Giants*, 122). She must have realized this as she prepared to return home and accordingly released the toad. Now James understands her on her own terms; he has an awareness of the difference of another person; and he seems to realize the truth of Mildred's injunction against becoming too involved in the lives of these people: individuals must make the important choices of their lives on their own. With this insight, James is ready to complete his own circular journey and return to his own bedroom.

Initially, the novel's concluding sentence appears ambiguous. After James looks around his room and ascertains the physical reality of his location, he lies back in his bed: "Very soon he was asleep again and dreaming a long, lovely dream about cosmonauts" (*Giants,* 123). Has he reverted to his love of science fiction and forgotten the significance of his journey with Mildred? Possibly. Norton, however, states that he is now dreaming, for the first time in the novel using that word in relation to his activities, and that he is on his own. He is not being guided by Mildred, an adult, into an alternate realm. He is a more mature individual than he was earlier that night, when Mildred had come to take him with her. Having understood the importance of that journey and having acted with courage on his own, he no longer needs her. In a sense, he has set the past in order and is now ready to face the future.

The stages of James's character development traced in the foregoing discussion are fairly typical of those found in the circular journey pattern.[2] Because of experiences on the journey, the individual returns to the point of departure changed. But what makes James's story unique, not just a slightly altered version of the same old story? Why does James travel to and from this specific location, to a land in which characters of well-known folktales and literary folktales live after their stories have ended, according to the formula, with them existing happily ever after? An approach to the answer may be found by examining a brief exchange between James and Mildred as they leave the castle early in the novel. When Mildred explains that fairy-tale characters live on "in the hearts of little children" (*Giants,* 26), James retorts, "They don't in mine" (*Giants,* 26). The key phrase in this exchange is "little children." James, who does not consider himself little, rejects fairy tales as being for small children. He does not recognize the people Mildred shows him as individuals, as is revealed by his categorization of Dulcibel as a standard story princess. He is even ignorant of the conventional aspects of these kinds of stories, as is apparent in his questions to Dulcibel when he meets her in the forest. To his query about how the spell came about, she offhandedly replies, "Oh, the usual way" (*Giants,* 68), the adjective ironically echoing his first impression of her. James's attitude toward these trips is typical of older children when they are taken by adults on outings they consider to be too childish for them.

Nevertheless, James has not been without a literary education in fairy tales. When Tabitha mentions Rumpelstiltskin, his "memory stir[s] faintly" (*Giants,* 74). And when Mildred chides him, saying that he must have heard of Big and Little Hans,

> A memory came back to James of a room in his grandmother's home, a small room, filled with books and sunlight. There had often been a patch of sunlight on the carpet, behind a large armchair that stood with its back to the window. That was where he would sit and read, his back against the shutters. A secret place. He remembered the dusty, fusty smell of the old book and the carpety smell of the carpet. It was a book that had belonged to his grandmother as a child. Some of the pages were missing. Yes, he remembered Big Hans and Little Hans. But he could not remember the story. (*Giants,* 43)

James will travel back to a place he had visited as a small child, the world of fairy tales, recovering what he had forgotten. He not only will meet the characters and learn the conventions but also will become actively involved in the stories, participating in events and, most important, understanding the human dimensions of the people. He will make story an integral part of his life. Not surprisingly, James feels "very shy and out of place" (*Giants,* 19) and uninterested in the salon where Mildred visits Boofy, Belle, and Pumpkin. He does not know or remember their stories; moreover, they are now dull, middle-aged people. The mention of a dragon killed by Beau is all that catches his attention. Only after he has talked with Dulcibel and entered the forest does he become involved, searching for the magical toad and then feeling admiration for the two Jacks. He does not, however, remember the old tales that well; if he had, he would have recalled that the old hero had killed only 12 giants and would have been much more puzzled than he is about the thirteenth tress.

James's character development, with its concomitant increase in his understanding of the various people with whom he interacts, can be seen as his rediscovery of the forgotten world of fairy tales and his new comprehension of the relationship between these stories and the realities of life. He cannot alter the endings of the tales, although he can, through his increased awareness of and sympathy for Dulcibel and the two Jacks, play a role in helping them to reach these endings. And the emotions with which he responds—joy, fear, courage, despair—can be brought back to his everyday world. His active response to the world of story can be important to him.

Mildred: The Storyteller as Fairy Godmother

Why Mildred? She is an author about whom the fairy-tale characters remark, "Who would remember us nowadays, dear Mildred, if you did not come?" (*Giants,* 14). While she now writes for a society magazine, reporting on these characters in the happily-ever-after period of their lives, she is also the adult who, by introducing children to traditional literature, keeps the stories alive from generation to generation. She is not unlike Mrs. May in *The Borrowers,* keeping the Clock family story alive by telling it to Kate. Although she sometimes seems annoyed at James's lack of interest or knowledge, she continues to take him with her on her various visits, as Mrs. May takes Kate to Bedfordshire, in *The Borrowers Afield,* reviving the girl's flagging interest in the story told two years earlier.

Yet Mildred's cryptic remarks about this trip suggest that she intends it to be a special one for the boy. She is evasive when he asks her if they will meet anyone dangerous; suggests that, in addition to his moccasins, he wear his leather jacket; is anxious to leave the palace; tells him: "[The people in the salon are] not the only ones . . . whom you're going to meet. . . . This may be rather exciting" (*Giants,* 25); and mentions several times, "We've so much to get through" (*Giants,* 35). She is eager to get to Much-Belungun-under-Bluff because "There's something there I'd like to see for myself. Since I was last there, there have been rumors" (*Giants,* 39). Yet when they arrive at the inn, she quickly decides to attend a royal wedding, appearing to have forgotten the rumors and not pressing James to accompany her, showing no uneasiness at leaving him behind for the first time. She returns to the inn only after the major adventures are over.

Why should she have departed so quickly, given her hints and her interest in the rumors about the village? It is tempting to attribute her actions to a flightiness of character and to label her a flibbertigibbet. Nonetheless, remembering that this is a novel drawing on characters and traditions of folklore, another explanation seems more plausible and appropriate. Perhaps Mildred is like the fairy godmothers of the old tales, the wise old persons who provide the heroes and heroines with the means and opportunities to help themselves. Displeased with James's intense—perhaps she thinks excessive—interest in the modern genre of science fiction, Mildred wishes to lead him to a discovery of the value of the stories he has forgotten. She can take him to the literature, but he must interact with it on his own. Again, she can be compared with Mrs. May, who leads Kate to the point at which the girl can tell the story.

Examined in light of this hypothesis, Mildred's actions up to the time of her departure from the inn take on new meaning. When she is about to go back to the salon to deliver an article she had apparently forgotten to give the women, she suggests that James play with Dulcibel, no doubt knowing that the girl would tell him her story, and she is happy to see that they have become friends. She may have left the gate unlocked so that the princess could follow them. In the forest, she offhandedly gives James directions to Hecubenna's house that he later follows. Her warning not to become too involved may be given to produce the opposite effect on the boy. She seems pleased that James likes the two Jacks, and by leaving on a perfectly understandable pretext, she gives James the opportunity to act without her. On her return, she expresses puzzlement on Dulcibel's mysterious disappearance from the castle. Has Mildred forgotten about the unlocked gate, or does she believe it best for James to be unaware of her guidance?

These hypotheses seem probable after examining Mildred's actions in comparison with those of Mrs. May in *The Borrowers* and *The Borrowers Afield*. That old woman, it will be recalled, had teased Kate into an interest in a story she knew, had helped the girl with the telling of the story, and then had withdrawn, enabling Kate to interact with Tom Goodenough, one of the principals, and to understand the actions and create her own meaning—to complete the narrative herself. Kate was unable to change how events had turned out, only to achieve fuller understanding of them and the characters. James cannot alter the resolution of Dulcibel's conflict. Mildred has insisted all along that her adventure would end the way it finally did. "I know the whole story," she tells him in the forest. "As you should . . . if you weren't so keen on science fiction" (*Giants,* 41). The whole story includes awareness of character motivation as well as events.

Of course, James finally does comprehend the whole story. In addition to realizing the right of Dulcibel to decide her own fate and admiring the courage she displays in doing so, he becomes aware of a vital aspect of human experience, one of considerable interest to Mildred: the way individuals deal with getting older. She had responded "a little too sharply" (*Giants,* 26) to his remark that the people at the court are so old. She spends much of her professional life keeping them alive in other people's minds and constantly comments on how well they are looking. But the fact remains that theirs are lives of ennui; they endure their days, and they feel helpless to do anything about the curse laid on Dulcibel. Beau, the only man James sees at the palace, is out of shape, and spends his days on sport hunting, killing inedible dragons and bland-tasting unicorns. By contrast, the humble characters try to lead worthwhile lives in the service of others. The two Hanses have an active livery business; the two Jacks are innkeepers. Moreover, Jack-the-Giant-Killer has destroyed not for sport, as does Beau, but to make the village safe from threatening beings. James comes to realize how distressed they feel at being "past it" (*Giants,* 78) and is delighted at their regained self-worth at growing the beanstalk and killing the final giant. Unlike the courtiers, whose lives seem to go on and on somewhat purposelessly, the Jacks, having achieved a satisfying closure to their stories, can live happily—and usefully—ever after in their old age.

Mildred is an antirevisionist storyteller. Unlike the many retellers of the nineteenth and twentieth centuries who have altered fairy tales so that events and characters are more in line with what they consider suitable for young readers, she believes that children should be given the opportunity to understand on their own the significance of these works as they are. That is why she leaves James alone to discover for himself the significance of the endings of Dulcibel's and the two Jacks' stories. The storyteller is thus a specialized wise old person performing for young readers what a fairy godperson does for the fairy-tale characters. Readers must be given the opportunity to fill in what German critic Wolfgang Iser has called the gaps in the text of a work of literature.[3] In that way, the traditional stories will continue to live and to be as relevant as some children think science fiction is. James, in bringing back his knowledge to his ordinary world, will have created a complete closure to this adventure of his life. He is like the active reader who gains personal as well as literary understanding from the stories. And Mildred, in making it possible for him to do so, is the ideal storyteller.

The Achievement of Mary Norton's *Tempest*

Are All the Giants Dead? is certainly not as good a book as *The Borrowers.* Somehow it lacks the intensity and vitality that make reading every page of that book such a delight. There are indeed pages that seem to move very slowly, causing the book to seem considerably longer than it is—just over 100 pages, much shorter than the four Borrowers books Norton had written up to that point. But the novel is no mean achievement. It is a very good book in many ways and can succeed on its own merits, without the influence of its author's name.

As noted, it marks an interesting variation on the literary genre of the dream journey, making James's trip one to an actual destination in an alternate sphere of reality. It is also a brave step for the author, away from the almost formulaic pattern she had established by the time she wrote *The Borrowers Aloft*. She shifts her gaze from a miniature world contained within a small part of Bedfordshire County to an entire kingdom extending from the palace of Boofy and Beau, through the woods, to Much-Belungun-under-Bluff, and finally to the plateau on which the giant's castle stands. Although the individual locations are not described in the minute detail that was characteristic of the Borrowers books, important settings are carefully detailed: the courtyard with its open well, the pond by the woodland clearing, the inn of the two Jacks, and the crevice up to the plateau. The settings are designed to provide a series of contrasts: the elegance of the palace and its occupants with the squalor around the giant's castle; the hominess of Hecubenna's cottage and the hospitable quality of the Jacks' inn with the somewhat frightening atmosphere of the woods.

Considerable humor lies in the book, from the portrayal of the middle-aged prince and princesses to the dialogue between James and Dulcibel. To James's question "Why do they always talk in rhyme?" the princess matter-of-factly replies: "It's the custom" (*Giants,* 68). When she says that the postern gate must have been opened by magic, his reply is equally matter-of-fact: "No, it wasn't magic. It was Mildred" (*Giants,* 70). On the bluff, he tells Dulcibel that if they are spotted by the giant, "[w]e'd be back down the crevice before he could say Jack Robinson," and is corrected by her: "Or Fee-fi-fo-fum. . . . That's more what they're supposed to say" (*Giants,* 95).

Perhaps Norton's major achievement is in her creation of a boy's adventure story with a difference. Unlike Mildred, Mary Norton is a revisionist storyteller. Although she has presented heroic boys in *Bed-Knob and Broomstick* and the Borrowers series, her focus was mainly on Carey and Miss Price in the former book and Arrietty, Homily, Kate, Mrs. May, and Miss Menzies in the latter books. Even the boy, who is the agency of both the Clock family's escape and of their story's transmission to his sister, is viewed from the outside, through Mrs. May's interpretation of him and her presentation of Arrietty's point of view in the direct narrative. By contrast, *Are All the Giants Dead?* is told from a limited third-person point of view that focuses on James's reaction to the characters and to the events in which he becomes involved. Norton's portrayal of aspects of his personality—his boredom, commonsense attitude to situations, practicality, kindness, and courage—are convincing. He is in many ways a typical boy, becoming most interested in the journey when there is mention of dragons, wolves, and giants. He is not fearless and totally independent: he frequently wishes that Mildred would return to assist him and Dulcibel in their difficult quest. The success of Norton's portrayal of his character makes readers' entry into the fantasy world easier, for average readers would be similar to James and would no doubt react in a manner like his.

James is, however, more than a vehicle for achieving credibility and a character to help readers become involved in the adventures. The story is mainly about how he reacts to the adventures. Significantly, he does not perform unlikely deeds, such as killing the thirteenth giant. This is not why he was taken into the fairy-tale land. He was provided with the opportunity of learning about himself and other people, of seeing himself in relationships. As such, *Are All the Giants Dead?* does not follow the adventure pattern delineated by Joseph Campbell in *The Hero with a Thousand Faces*.[4] Slaying a dragon is not the issue. Sensitively understanding, responding to, and helping—but not controlling—others is what makes James, like Charles in *Bonfires and Broomsticks* and Mrs. May's brother in *The Borrowers,* a heroic boy. *Are All the Giants Dead?* is a woman writer's sensitive and detailed examination and analysis of the nature of a boy's important steps toward maturity. This is the author's major achievement as a revisionist storyteller.

Finally, the novel can be related to the author herself. As noted, many of the adult characters, particularly the two Jacks, are concerned about being "past it" (*Giants,* 78). Jack-the-Giant-Killer worried not only that he had lost his special skill but also that he could no longer provide a valuable service to his fellow villagers. Such a life would be virtually worthless, as are the lives of Boofy and Beau, Belle, and Pumpkin. Even Mildred seems worried about being ineffective, as is indicated by her annoyance at James's remark about the courtiers being old. She is obviously pleased that the fairy-tale characters appreciate her "society columns" and wishes she was having more effect on James, impatiently telling him, "I don't know anything about science fiction! I can only take you where I can take you. You mustn't be ungrateful" (*Giants,* 26). As events prove, neither the two Jacks nor Mildred are "past it."

Mildred has helped James to appreciate the values of the stories he had forgotten and considered somewhat disdainfully. Perhaps she is a persona of Mary Norton herself. With the exception of the short, relatively trivial

Poor Stainless, she had published nothing in the 14 years since *The Borrowers Aloft,* the fourth and apparently final volume of the Borrowers series. Had Mary Norton too lost her touch? As *Are All the Giants Dead?* indicates, she had not. She created a novel that is not only an engaging story with convincing characters and an intriguing plot but also a testimony to the value of stories and storytelling. Although she was to return to the Borrowers in a fifth novel, she has written in *Are All the Giants Dead?* a kind of *Tempest,* (apparently) a final work that, like Shakespeare's play and William Faulkner's *The Reivers,* is a rich and mellow closure to her career as an author, a summation of her attitudes to the relationship between life and story. As British critic Margery Fisher wrote of the novel, "Every word counts, every piece of talk or description deserves renewed attention, however simple it may appear" (Senick, 225).

Chapter Six

Of Her Times and for All Time

The Achievement of Mary Norton

As both contemporary and continuing critical and popular responses to Mary Norton's children's novels reveal, she was quickly recognized as and is still considered to be one of the most significant British children's writers of the midtwentieth century. While her achievement is unique, it shares qualities with those of many major writers. Mary Norton is very much a writer of her own times, responding to the biographical, social, and literary aspects of both her early twentieth-century childhood, the temporal setting of her Borrowers series, and midcentury Britain, during which she created most of her children's books. She also dealt with aspects of storytelling and human nature that, nearly half a century later, speak not only to British children but also to children and adults in many other countries as well. While it may be too early to make a definitive evaluation of her work, it is not too early to say that her enduring qualities result from her ability to write with insight, grace, and charm about and from her own times and for all time.

Norton and the Golden Age of Children's Literature

The biographical sketch of Mary Norton included in chapter 1 noted some similarities between her novels and those of the Golden Age of Children's Literature, the period between 1870 and the beginning of World War I in 1914. In addition to these similarities, many others can be mentioned. The failing belief and interest in earlier magical or wondrous experiences felt by the central characters at the beginning of George Macdonald's *The Princess and Curdie* (1882) parallel the situations of the Wilson children and Kate in the first chapters of *Bonfires and Broomsticks* and *The Borrowers Afield*, respectively. Like Wendy in Sir James Matthew Barrie's *Peter Pan* (1911), Homily almost immediately begins tidying up each new dwelling the Clock family enters. Arrietty and the boy's sharing secrets against adults in *The Borrowers* is like the activities of Mary Lennox and Colin Craven in Frances Hodgson

Burnett's *The Secret Garden* (1911). Mole's springtime cleanup and emergence from his home and joyous response to the riverbank world he discovers, seen in the first chapter of Kenneth Grahame's *The Wind in the Willows* (1908), can be compared to Arrietty's first May-morning trip from beneath the clock and into the outdoors.

While noticing these and other parallels does not prove that Norton had read and been influenced by the great works of the Golden Age, it does provide a way of seeing the uniqueness of her achievement. Setting the Borrowers series in a time in which these works were most widely read and creating in many of her books situations and characters similar to ones found in these Golden Age books, Norton nonetheless creates a very different world from theirs, one which reflects the struggles and uncertainties of the times in which she wrote. The relationship between *Bed-Knob and Broomstick* and the short story collections of E. Nesbit has been traced in chapter 2; however, Nesbit's books emphasized not only the adventures of the children, but also the stability of the homes from which they departed and to which they returned, or that of the new ones at which they finally arrived. Although the Wilson children return to their home at the end of each of the two novels of *Bed-Knob and Broomstick,* the first emphasizes the dangers of their final destination, wartime London, and the latter focuses on Miss Price's marriage and departure for the seventeenth century. The first to fourth books of the Borrowers series, of course, deal with the loss of homes, while the fifth ends with at best a tenuous sense of the security of the Clocks' new home. Only in *Are All the Giants Dead?* is a return home emphasized, as James awakens in his own bedroom. But the implication is that he has made his last journey with Mildred who, like Miss Price for Carey Wilson, he will not see again. Moreover, his dream of cosmonauts is futuristic, suggesting new directions in which his imagination will travel.

In *The Borrowers Afield* and *The Borrowers Afloat* are found many similarities to Kenneth Grahame's *The Wind in the Willows,* the most important of which deal with riverbank homes. As critics have frequently noted, Grahame's River Bank represents an ideal environment, a contrast to both the natural savagery of the Wild Wood and the civilized chaos of the Wide World. Mole's migration to it is necessary if he is to mature; Rat's failed attempt to leave it is seen as a near violation of his being; Toad's catastrophes occur when he leaves it. The tour boats that pass by pose little threat, and floods do no serious damage to Rat's home. The central males will spend long, happy, and contented adult bachelorhoods in this setting.

By contrast, the stream by which the Clocks make first their boot home and later their kettle home offers little security. These are not permanent and the river is not an idyllic setting. Although Pod and Homily work ingeniously to make each temporary dwelling as comfortable as possible, each is vulnerable to animals and floods and, more important, to human eyes. In *The Borrowers Afield,* Mild Eye discovers his boot, and as a result, the Clocks are briefly trapped in his caravan. In *The Borrowers Afloat,* the dislodged kettle spins dangerously down the flooded stream and becomes stuck on a floating island, where the Clocks are again seen by Mild Eye. Indeed, each of the family's riverbank adventures is fraught with danger, a fact that emphasizes the vulnerability and homelessness of Pod, Homily, and Arrietty. Writing in part about Arrietty's movement through the uncertainties of adolescence and against the background of both the author's frequent moves in the 1930s and 1940s and the unsettling conditions of England during and after World War II, Norton could not find in the symbol of riverbank life the same sense of security, contentment, and changelessness that Grahame, perhaps an escapist from conditions of the urbanized, adult worlds of his time, could.

An important conversation between Arrietty and the boy during their first encounter reveals interesting parallels and differences between the Borrowers series and *Peter Pan.* When the boy asks Arrietty if she can fly, she retorts that she is not a fairy and says, "I don't believe in them" (*Borrowers,* 76). Although he seems to be surprised by her reply, he quickly, as if to save face, says that he does not either. Arrietty then goes on to repeat her mother's account of a fairy she thought she once saw: "About the size of a glowworm with wings like a butterfly. And it had a tiny little face, she said, all alight and moving like sparks and tiny moving hands. Its face was changing all the time, she said, smiling and sort of shimmering. It seemed to be talking, she said, very quickly—but you couldn't hear a word" (*Borrowers,* 77).

Her mother's fairy is very similar to Barrie's Tinker Bell. Given the approximate date of the events in Norton's story, 1910, it seems probable that the boy, who is familiar with London concerts, had seen the play *Peter Pan* and been one of the thousands of children who had helped to revive Tinker Bell through their belief in fairies. The situation of the large boy talking to the tiny Arrietty parallels that between Peter and Tinker Bell.

By implicitly drawing readers' attention to parallels with *Peter Pan,* Norton invites them to consider both the similarities and the differences in the characters, situations, and themes of the two novels. Each considers the question of belief. Tinker Bell can survive only with it. Interestingly, she dies a few years after the Darlings' visit to Never-Never-Land and is immediately forgotten by Peter. He will not be able to tell subsequent girls about her, and memory of her existence will be lost to the human characters in Barrie's fictional world. Such is not the case for Arrietty and her family. Because he believes in the reality of the Clock family, the boy initiates a chain of belief extending over the years from himself to his sister, to Kate, and then, through her writing the story down, to her daughters, and, as long as her written record lasts, to her descendants.

The similarity of the relationships between Arrietty and the boy and Peter and Tinker Bell ends with the size disparity. Peter remains a child in his manipulative power relationship with the short-lived but sexually much more mature fairy. The boy, however, matures because of his friendship with Arrietty and develops a mutually beneficial relationship with her. Coldly indifferent in many of his responses to Tinker Bell, Peter acts mainly to feed his monstrous ego. The boy's genuine act of courage is selflessly taken at great risk for himself. He does not cease to remember Arrietty, still talking about her when he becomes an adult.

With the introduction of Spiller into the story, a second significant echo of Peter Pan occurs in *The Borrowers Afield*. Like Peter, Spiller is first seen on the outside, looking in on a domestic scene: the Clocks settling into their temporary boot home. Also, like Peter's, Spiller's clothing makes him a part of nature, and, at first, he is almost amoral in his dealings with the family. Unlike Peter, however, Spiller quickly develops a sense of responsibility for his new friend. Moreover, he matures, becomes a part of the Clock family, and, as the epilogue to *The Borrowers Aloft* notes, marries Arrietty and establishes a home. He becomes what Peter can never become.

Finally, it should be noted that unlike Wendy, who returns to the Darling home having undergone a maturing process as a result of her adventure, Arrietty never returns to Firbank Hall. In fact, she must leave Firbank in order to mature. Writing at midcentury, when a shifting society was making the permanence of a home increasingly rare, Norton does not appropriate those elements of a classic which are, among other things, an examination of the homing instinct. Wendy is also different from Kate, whose belief in the Borrowers is so great that, years later, she preserves their memory in a story written for her children. Perhaps the only sense of permanence Norton can imagine is memory as provided through story.

Norton and Midtwentieth-Century Children's Literature

While in its detailed portrayal of the lives of tiny people the Borrowers series belongs to a tradition extending in English literature at least back to Jonathan Swift's eighteenth-century classic *Gulliver's Travels* (1726), it invites closer comparison with a book published in 1947, only five years before *The Borrowers:* T. H. White's *Mistress Masham's Repose.* There are no explicit references to that book in the Borrowers series, nor did Mary Norton refer to it in any of her statements about her writing career. Yet given the popularity of White as a children's and adult writer (his *The Sword in the Stone,* published in 1938, quickly became a classic) and the similarity of the basic premise of *Mistress Masham's Repose*—tiny people living in a human-size world—to Norton's professed childhood imaginings about little people, it is difficult to believe that she was unaware of White's novel or that it did not, even in a slight way, influence the formation of her own best-known works.

There are many similarities of plot, parallels between characters, resemblances of incidents, and congruities of themes in *Mistress Masham's Repose* and the Borrowers series. Both White's novel and *The Borrowers* are set in and around once prosperous country mansions. Living close to the few remaining human beings are little people of whom the human beings are unaware. In fact, their being undiscovered is essential to the little people's well-being, and the plots begin when they are sighted by human beings. Both plots involve the capture of little people by power-seeking adults and the developing relationships between a human child and these beings. Many characters in the works of the two authors are similar: the lonely children, Maria and the boy; the dominating Miss Brown, the governess, and Mrs. Driver; Mr. Hater, the vicar, and Mr. Platter, both of whom wear thick glasses that cover their eyes; and Gradgnag, the master trapper, and Spiller.

Perhaps the most important similarities between White's and Norton's novels are the themes developed around the human beings' attitudes toward the little people, the Lilliputians and the Borrowers, they encounter. Maria, like the boy, Tom Goodenough, and Miss Menzies, experiences conflicts between feelings of love for and proprietorship toward her newfound friends. Her human friend, the somewhat befuddled professor, clarifies the problem for her: "If they love you . . . very well. You may love them. But do you think, Maria, that you can make them love you for yourself alone, by wrapping prisoners up in dirty handkerchiefs?"[1] As Pod told Arrietty at the conclusion of *The Borrowers Aloft,* human beings, no matter how well intentioned, can bring only sorrow to the Borrowers in whose lives they interfere. Similarly, "Maria's misfortunes . . . dated from the night on which she had interfered" (White, 82). Her character becomes stronger as she respects her Lilliputian friends and allows them their autonomy. Miss Brown and Mr. Hater, who refers to what Maria calls "the People" as "mannikins," do not recognize their integrity and wish to capture them, to violate their dignity, all for personal profit, as do Mild Eye, the gypsy, and Mr. and Mrs. Platter in the Borrowers series.

Despite these similarities, many differences exist between the authors' portrayals of the Lilliputians and the Borrowers, differences that help to clarify the uniqueness of Mary Norton's achievement. First, the sociology and history of the Lilliputians and the Borrowers are dissimilar. The former are descendants of tiny people captured from the island visited by Lemuel Gulliver in book 1 of *Gulliver's Travels.* They have lived for 300 moons on a tiny island, Mistress Masham's Repose, independent of and undiscovered by human beings. In fact, the decline in the fortune of the great estate has aided them in remaining hidden. Exceeding 500 in number, they have developed an intricate culture based on that of eighteenth-century England, a culture that will continue as long as their presence is unknown. The Borrowers, by contrast, have always depended on the human beings in whose houses they have lived, not only adapting the human materials they "borrow" but also imitating the manners of those human beings whom they most frequently observe. In a sense, Homily and Pod are closer to Mrs. Driver and Crampfurl than they realize. The decline of the prosperity of Firbank Hall has led to hard times for Borrowers; all but the Clock family have left. Emigration, as Arrietty realizes, is necessary for the continuance of the race. Firbank Hall no longer contains a complete society, only a family.

Whereas *Mistress Masham's Repose* focuses on the human child Maria, tracing the moral growth she undergoes in her relationship with her tiny friends, the Borrowers series is largely Arrietty's story, a bildungsroman that involves her necessary disassociation from the human beings she befriends. At the conclusion of her story, Maria is still a child, financially secure and still in frequent contact with the Lilliputians. Arrietty, on the edge of womanhood, will no doubt marry Spiller, entering an adult relationship with one of her own species, in which the future of the species will be ensured. She has forsworn all future contact with her human friends. Norton is deeply concerned with portraying Arrietty as a developing individual; White's adult Lilliputians are at best static character types. Moreover, Norton, a female author, presents the female psychology of Arrietty in great detail; Maria, created by a male author, is almost a generic child-orphan.

Finally, although *Mistress Masham's Repose* and *The Borrowers* are both told by an adult to a child, the former lacks the frame narrative and consequently the importance of the narrator to the meaning of the story. Amaryllis, the recipient of White's story, may be intended to learn about the immorality of power relationships, but she is never present, and the purpose of her being the specific audience is neither stated nor implied. By contrast, as discussed earlier, Kate's reactions to Mrs. May's narrative—reactions that may have been provoked by the older woman—are central to the meaning of *The Borrowers*. Mrs. May is a woman talking to a girl, telling a story that focuses mainly on females.

Thus, although White's and Norton's books share many similarities, their differences are also many and are more significant. Examination of these help to indicate the specific achievement of Mary Norton as a children's writer. From the publication of *The Magic Bed-Knob,* she had worked within but considerably modified established genres of children's literature. White's portrayal of and examination into the lives of the Lilliputions are both very similar to and highly dependent on Swift's *Gulliver's Travels.* It is more a sequel to than an adaptation or revision of that work. The portrayal of Maria seems to be White's major original contribution, and even that may have been influenced by the portrait of Glumdalclitch, the giant Brobdignagian girl of book 2 of Swift's classic. With the exception of Mild Eye's attempts to capture the Clocks (mainly plot devices intended to set up escapes), the place Mary Norton's work seems most to resemble the Swiftian tradition and White's use of it is in the discussion of the Platters' attempts to display the Clock family in *The Borrowers Aloft* and *The Borrowers Avenged.* Yet even in these books, more attention is paid to Arrietty's ongoing maturation, particularly her understanding of her relationship with her parents, Spiller, Peagreen, and her human friend Miss Menzies.

The technique of describing the physical surroundings of the Clock family may owe something to book 2 of *Gulliver's Travels,* in which the hero responds to a world that is huge to him. This is in contrast to *Mistress Masham's Repose,* which, in its physical descriptions, is closer to book 1. However Swiftian Norton's descriptive technique may be, the concept of the Borrowers, as well as the characters and their lives, is her own. The idea of a tiny species dependent on the very human beings whom they must avoid provided the basis for plots that emphasize the precariousness of the Clocks' life. The conflicts between Arrietty and her parents, the resolutions of which signal her developing maturity, and the thematic discussions emerging out of the ways human beings react to seeing the Borrowers are her own. The extensive narrative frameworks of the first three books in the series, the choice of narrators, and the link between the frameworks and the narrative are also unique, examples of Norton's technical contributions to the children's novel.

The Borrowers series invites comparison with another series published during the same period as Norton's, Lucy M. Boston's Green Knowe novels. The central symbol of the six books, which appeared between 1954 and 1976, is Green Knowe, a nine-centuries-old Norman building that is now the home of the aging Mrs. Oldknow. Its dominant characteristics are its antiquity, its continuity, and most important, its essential timelessness. The words Boston used to describe her own home can be applied to it: "Inside, partly because of the silence within the massive stone walls, partly because of the complexity of the incurving shapes, you get a unique impression of time as a co-existent whole."[2] The building materials of the house, "all dating back to the day of creation, when God made the earth,"[3] possess qualities that have existed since the beginning of time. In many ways, the house and its environs are a kind of refuge. Those who approach it in the proper spirit can experience a timelessness that does not exist beyond its boundaries. They can come into contact with the "truth about being and knowing"[4] that emanates from the house and is absent from the outside world, where, as one character notes, "civilization moves so fast you can't travel fast enough to keep up with it."[5]

Adults cannot generally respond to this place as fully as children, and not all children can with equal success. The first two books of the series, *The Children of Green Knowe* and *The Chimneys of Green Knowe,* describe the steps by which Tolly, Mrs. Oldknow's great-grandson, enters into, understands, and becomes a part of this world, making contact with ancestors from the seventeenth and eighteenth centuries and taking actions to preserve the home's safety. In *A Stranger at Green Knowe* and *An Enemy at Green Knowe,* the fourth and fifth books of the series, Green Knowe is seriously but unsuccessfully threatened: in the former, by the forces of modern, mechanized civilization; in the latter, by universal powers of evil. *The Stones of Green Knowe,* published 12 years after the fifth novel, brings the series to a conclusion and a satisfying closure. In it, Roger, an occupant of the house when it was first built, visits children who have lived in it at various times and sees it survive various destructive forces. At the novel's end, he gathers with these children and Mrs. Oldknow, now transformed into a girl. She gives him a ring, which, she notes, will return through the ages to her. In so doing, she creates an inviolable circle of time.

This brief outline of the plots of Boston's novels suggests the common themes shared by the two series, both written in a midcentury era of change but different in their resolutions. Like Arrietty and her family, the children of Green Knowe must face the threats to a way of life that had altered little for generations. But whereas the children of Green Knowe retreat into a timeless world symbolized by the old home, one challenged but ultimately unaltered by outside forces, Arrietty must leave Firbank Hall forever, learning along with her parents how to survive under new conditions. In their retreat, the children of Green Knowe can remain forever in a world of innocence; Arrietty must grow into adulthood. Whereas Boston creates a closure in which the story can constantly reenact itself in an eternal circle, with the children safe in their knowledge of that circle, Norton creates an uneasy closure. Arrietty is entering a new phase of existence. Unlike Boston's characters, she is no longer a child, and she and her family can never, as Peagreen notes in the series' final words, count on certain safety. Stories, as Mrs. May says, go "on and on and on" (*Borrowers,* 158); they move linearly into the future. For Boston, in effect, stories go around and around endlessly in a sphere in which past, present, and future exist simultaneously. For Norton, certainty is not possible; for Boston, it can be achieved. Norton, with qualified optimism about the future, has her characters advance; Boston, disillusioned by the present, has them retreat. Perhaps that is why Arrietty is presented as a growing, developing character, while the children of Green Knowe are relatively static.[6]

One aspect that the two series do share is their presentation of old women telling stories to young children, stories that relate to the past and are of particular value in helping the listeners deal with their own lives. In the Green Knowe books, Mrs. Oldknow, whose name is symbolic, is not, until the final book, directly involved with her great-grandson's encounters with his ancestors. She is a mentor, telling him stories of the past and encouraging him to use his imaginative powers to assist him in making contact with that past. In *The Chimneys of Green Knowe,* Tolly decides to find lost family jewels to help his great-grandmother retain possession of her ancient home; however, he must first learn more about the past. Thus, he hears more of Mrs. Oldknow's legends in the evenings, as Grand, as he calls her, repairs a very old patchwork quilt. As had been the case for Kate and Mrs. May in *The Borrowers,* the act of sorting out pieces of cloth and sewing the quilt serves as a metaphor for the restoration and re-creation of the past through storytelling. Both storytellers are conservators of the past, not mere entertainers or historians but women who seek to make this past important in the lives of their child audiences. Mrs. Oldknow, though, has a vested interest in that past; in telling the stories to Tolly, she is making it possible for him to save her home from the threats of the present. In part because he is such a good listener, Tolly is able to enter into the timeless world of Green Knowe. In contrast, Mrs. May, recognizing similarities between her auditor and the central character of her narrative, decides to tell the story to Kate partly so that, through hearing the bildungsroman, her young listener will be assisted in her own growth process. Both Kate and Arrietty leave their pasts, their childhoods, behind. Interestingly enough, Mrs. Oldknow is seen as a child near the end of the final novel, *The Stones of Green Knowe,* whereas Mrs. May disappears early in *The Borrowers Afloat,* the third volume of that series. Kate's need for her is over.

Mrs. Oldknow can also be contrasted to Mildred, the male hero's guide in *Are All the Giants Dead?* Like Tolly, who in his trips to the past becomes one of the actors, the unknown individual of one of Mrs. Oldknow's stories, James becomes involved in the lives of the fairy-tale characters Mildred has introduced him to. But whereas Tolly has a direct influence on his ancestral history, James is at best a catalyst in the old stories, the plots of which remain unchanged. His trip to the land of the fairy-tale characters is a smaller circular journey in his linear progress toward maturity.[7]

Norton's Social and Psychological Vision

The examination of underlying differences in similar themes, characters, and events in Mary Norton's novels and those of other children's books reveals not only her literary uniqueness but the nature of her vision of English life in the first half of this century. Set in the time in which it was written, *Bed-Knob and Broomstick* reflects the traumas of life in England during World War II. The security available to E. Nesbit's Bastable children is not available to the Wilsons. Set in the Edwardian era of illusory peace and tranquillity, the Borrowers series reveals the profoundly disruptive underlying changes taking place at the time. In

Are All the Giants Dead? James, a child of the 1970s, discovers that even the perfect closures of traditional stories are false.

Of the Borrowers series, British critic Gillian Avery has written, "Adults may read the five books as a parable of . . . the wanderings of the homeless and the stateless of this century."[8] Mary Norton herself, in the introduction to *The Borrowers Omnibus,* published in 1966, invites such an approach: "It was only just before the 1940 war, when a change was creeping over the world as we had known it, that one thought about the Borrowers. There were human men and women who were being forced to live (by stark and tragic necessity) the kind of lives a child had once envisaged for a race of mythical creatures" (*Omnibus,* x). Several critics of the past decade have examined in detail the relationship between the books and their sociopolitical background. The Rustins see in the five volumes parallels to the decline of the landed gentry before World War II, the destruction of British homes during the Blitz, and the "petit bourgeois ambition" (Rustin and Rustin, 72) and consumerism in the decade after the war. For Nigel Hand, the series reflects "the dissolution of the class structure . . . [and] the pains of social mobility in a techno-logical society" (Hand, 51). Each notes Norton's criticism of many of the aspects of modern life, as does Kuznets, who considers Norton a sup-porter of the traditional work ethic and a rejecter of the welfare state (Kuznets 1985a, 201).

No doubt these elements can be found in Mary Norton's novels. Like those of most writers, her works are an outgrowth of and response to her times, as she has experienced and observed them. Much of the immedia-cy and intensity of the characters and events she depicts draw from this source. But to see the books as allegorical representations of aspects of twentieth-century British life is to recognize only one facet of her work. In an important but seldom noticed statement about her writing, Norton draws attention to another dimension of her work: "[I]t has something of the whole human dilemma—a microcosm of our world and the powers which rule us. In each generation, only youth is restless and brave enough to try to get out from 'under the floorboards'" (Commire, 239). Within the framework of British life in the first half of the twentieth century, Norton, in each of her novels, presents the recur-rent story of a young person's growth to maturity. Her works are bil-dungsromans, narratives of rites of passage that belong to story traditions extending back to the folktales, legends, and myths of most preliterate cultures. Charles and Carey Wilson, Arrietty and the boy, and James and Dulcibel struggle to define who they are and where they belong in a world that for them has lost many of its certainties. Coming of age is always a difficult process; in the eras of which Norton writes and in which she lived it is especially so.

Arrietty's story is the most detailed—perhaps not surprising when one considers the author's gender. Even so, three of the children who grow most fully are males: Charles Wilson, the boy, and James. Each shares in common a sensitive nature: Charles is timid; the boy feels inferior to his sisters; and James, otherwise very average, is unsure without Mildred, and, like the boy, weeps over the misfortunes of his friends. Yet each is capable of a quiet heroism in which he loses concern for himself and acts for others. None slay dragons or giants, as was the fashion in much popular boys' fiction. Mary Norton has, then, revised the male coming-of-age story and redefined the notion of male heroism. Sensitivity toward and respect for others' well-being becomes the standard by which she measures heroism and maturity. Her maturing boys are not Jacks-of-the-Beanstalk or St. Georges.

Nor is Arrietty, like the author almost a "tomboy," depicted in the mold of most females found in girls' novels of the nineteenth and earlier twentieth centuries. Her development is, however, surprisingly consistent with patterns analyzed by recent feminist critics and psychologists. The changes Arrietty undergoes, marked by both insecurity and rebelliousness, leave her with a far better understanding of herself in relation to the traditions of the past—embodied in part in her parents—and the complex and shifting world beyond the floorboards of Firbank Hall. A child growing up in the Edwardian age, she is not unlike the adult heroines of such contemporary women novelists as Doris Lessing, Margaret Atwood, and Toni Morrison. Or, as some feminist critics might say, Norton has stripped away the stereotypical notions of women fostered by generations of patriarchal control to reveal the authentic nature of female experience.

One of Mary Norton's most significant contributions to the coming-of-age genre is her emphasis on the significance of children's relationships to adults during the maturation process. In many children's stories, particularly several from the Golden Age, adults are frequently absent. Often they practice a kind of benign neglect, like Albert-next-door's uncle in E. Nesbit's *The Story of the Treasure Seekers* (1899), who is in the distant background, offering an invisible sense of security and, occasionally, wise advice. Sometimes the children are on summer vacations, free from adult control and scrutiny. Usually the adults involved in the actions are what Kenneth Grahame termed Olympians, powerful, repressive individuals imposing their will on small and younger beings. Some of these types are present in Norton's novels. Aunt Beatrice, in *The Magic Bed-Knob*, and Mrs. Driver, in *The Borrowers*, are Olympians. Miss Price, in the first half of *The Magic Bed-Knob,* and Mildred, in *Are All the Giants Dead?* exercise benign neglect. In most instances, however, the children grow partly because they understand the strengths and weakness of the adults with whom they interact. In *Bonfires and Broomsticks,* Carey, who has become deeply fond of Miss Price, realizes the spinster's loneliness and works hard to effect a match between her and Emelius Jones. Arrietty, aware of her parents' limitations, comes to understand both the causes of these and Pod and Homily's very real character strengths. One of the greatest obstacles to Arrietty's achievement of adulthood is the unresolved conflict she experiences between her loyalty to Miss Menzies, whose friendship and sadness she feels, and her parents' demands that she forever break off contact with human beings. Painful though it is for her, she accepts their will, having perceived the correctness of their adult wisdom and its applicability to her own adult life. In *Are All the Giants Dead?* James feels an immediate affinity to the aging Jacks, understands their feelings of failure, and provides them with information that leads to their final heroic achievement, the slaying of the last giant.

Yet the children also surpass the adults. For the Jacks, after the death of the giants "[t]he story . . . had ended" (*Giants,* 116). Not so for James; only when he has accepted Dulcibel's right to freedom of choice is he ready to return to his own world. Having left the world of fairy tales behind, he enters the futuristic world of science fiction, a realm that his mentor Mildred has admitted she does not understand. While Arrietty understands the wisdom of her parents' advice, she leaves behind the rigid, household rules of borrowing, entering imaginatively and creatively into literal and symbolic new worlds they still fear. Even Kate, who in *The Borrowers* has been led by Mrs. May into a wondrous realm she had not known before, goes much further than the old woman, learning facts about the Borrowers' lives that Mrs. May had never dreamed of.

What the children in Mary Norton's novels possess that allows them to surpass the adults in their lives is what Hand has called "freely-creative imagination" (Hand, 45). Because they are able to respond to the possibilities of friendship with Miss Price, the Wilson children escape from their confining life with Aunt Beatrice. Arrietty is able to move beyond the physical and psychologically restricting subfloorboard life of her parents because she can envision a life of freedom in nature. Her greatest imaginative leap may be her ability to perceive the relationship between articles about ballooning she is reading in the *Illustrated London News* and a means of escape from the attic in which the Platters have locked her family. In contrast to the aging courtiers and even the two Jacks of *Are All the Giants Dead?* James develops an ability to react imaginatively to the situations he encounters. Not that all the adults are totally incapable of changing and of responding imaginatively: Miss Price, Pod and Homily, Mr. Potts, and even the two Jacks do change and see ways of adapting their lives to the new circumstances in which they find themselves. But writing for children as she is, Norton focuses on young characters, examining their maturation in part as it relates to their imaginative responses to their world.

The Value of Creative Response to Story

Much of the young characters' imaginative response is found in the way they relate to the stories they hear. Arrietty has heard from Homily many tales of her mother's childhood and the family mythology. She reacts sensitively, imagining the quality of the lives of the Overmantels, finding in the disappeared Eggletina a role model, and realizing that the disappearance of the once large Borrower society may mean the end of her race. The knowledge and understanding she gains from the stories fuel her desire to leave the confines of her childhood world. She becomes a storyteller as well, relating the family history to the boy, the adventures afield to Tom Goodenough, and a variety of tales to her little cousin Timmis. Not only does her telling keep the memory of her family and race alive, but in the boy's case, it helps him to move beyond the self-centered perspectives of his childhood. He in turn becomes a storyteller, a link in the ongoing chain of narrative transmission. Within the narrative framework of the Borrowers series, Kate matures. From a listener to Mrs. May, she becomes a coteller and later the sole teller of the Clocks' saga, moving beyond her older relative in her knowledge and understanding of characters and events. James too grows because of his contact with stories. Although he had almost sullenly responded to Mildred that the people of the old fairy tales do not live in his memory, he soon becomes intimately involved in their lives.

One of Norton's major achievements is in her presentation of the theme of the nature and importance of stories and storytelling, a theme found occasionally in children's novels but one central to such adult novelists as William Faulkner, Isabel Allende, and Timothy Findley. Like these writers, Norton believes that the telling of stories is a means of preserving the past, making it still live in the present, and an important shaping influence in the lives of those who continue to tell and listen to stories.[9] Both the listeners in the novels and the readers of them are not expected to be passive recipients of the narratives; they are called on to be re-creators and cocreators. When the Wilsons report their first misadventure to Miss Price, they "often interrupted each other, and sometimes they spoke in chorus, but gradually Miss Price pieced the pattern together. She became graver and graver" (*Bed-Knob,* 57). Out of what she hears, Miss Price creates a story, makes meaning, and responds to it, gradually becoming more deeply involved in the Wilson's lives. Such is also true of the boy, Kate, and James. And Norton seems to expect or even demand similar activities on the part of her readers.

In many ways, Norton's novels, particularly those in the Borrowers series, meet the criteria for superior works of literature advanced by the French literary theorist Roland Barthes. He stated that good writers create "texts" rather than "works," that these are "scriptible" rather than "lisible," and that readers of them experience *"jouissance"* rather than pleasure. The term *scriptible* suggests that the piece of literature is not complete in its published form; it is "rewritten" by readers, who create their own novel from the author's words and experience a creative joy in the activity rather than a passive pleasure.[10] Certainly, that is what Arrietty does with Homily's stories, the boy with Arrietty's, Mrs. May's with his, and Kate with hers. Even Kate must re-create the story that she and Mrs. May had cocreated at the end of *The Borrowers,* interacting with new texts—Arrietty's written *Diary* and Tom Goodenough's oral recollections—to write down her story for her children. Norton finally casts doubts on the fictional accuracy of events in her own novels, leading readers to question and to come up with their own answers to some vexing problems. Why did Mrs. May tell the story to Kate, and did she interpret events in the light of her own life? Why did she question the authenticity of the text of the miniature memorandum book she claimed to have found? If *The Borrowers Afield* reveals the inaccuracy of her hypotheses about the events of the Clocks' escape from Firbank Hall, how accurate is the narrative Kate writes for her children? By responding actively and imaginatively to these implied questions, readers are using elements of their own personal and literary experiences to create new versions of the stories, and they are making the stories an integral and important part of their own lives. Not only are the novels of Mary Norton interesting and exciting reading; they can become forces assisting readers in their own development in and response to the worlds in which they live.

These elements in the works of Mary Norton would have little significance had her novels been poorly written. But they were not: Norton was a superb writer. The adventures of the Clock family are presented in a fast-paced, exciting manner. The many dangers the family experience are vividly realized. With the exception of such a minor character as the cannibal witch doctor in *The Magic Bed-Knob,* the characters are well developed. The members of the Clock family and the people they meet, human and Borrower, reflect the varied aspects of human nature. Even the villains, the Olympian adults who seek to repress the Borrowers, are presented in some detail. Mrs. Driver's quest for power and control is partly a result of her vulnerability as a member of the servant class. Marginalized by English society, Mild Eye, the gypsy, is driven to steal; he is not malicious toward the Clock family—he sees them as a means of acquiring wealth like that he views in his wanderings. Mr. Platter has fallen on hard times, a victim of the modern world he has literally helped to build. The loneliness of such adults as Mrs. May and Miss Menzies, as well as Mildred's need to feel useful as she grows older, is portrayed with sensitivity and kindness. Mary Norton has created her characters with the same loving care and attention to detail that Mr. Pott gave to making the figures in his model village.

This skill of characterization contributes a great deal to the convincing quality of Mary Norton's literally improbable fictions. Equally important is her meticulous attention to the physical details of the objects and settings of the stories, from the contrasting appearances of Miss Price's and Emelius Jones's laboratories, to the dwellings of the Borrowers, to the inn run by the two Jacks.

The eagerness with which readers awaited the appearance of the sequels of Mary Norton's two series or a new, completely different book from her pen attests to her great skill as a storyteller. The frequency with which many readers returned to individual titles, the emergence of new and enthusiastic readers in ensuing decades, and the growing body of perceptive and appreciative criticism are a tribute to the lasting qualities of her work. Mary Norton wrote sensitively and clearly about her own era, dealt with themes that have assumed greater importance in the later years of the twentieth century, and presented children's concerns that may well be timeless. She is truly a children's writer of her times and for all time.

Notes

Chapter One

1. Mary Norton, *The Borrowers Afield* (New York: Harcourt, Brace, 1955), 3; hereafter cited in text as *Afield.*
2. Carol Price, "A Life in the Day of Mary Norton," *Sunday Times Magazine,* 31 October 1982, 97.
3. Richard Wildman, *Victorian and Edwardian Bedfordshire from Old Photographs* (London: B. T. Batsford, 1978), n.p.
4. Mary Norton, *The Borrowers* (New York: Harcourt, Brace, 1953), 86; hereafter cited in text as *Borrowers.*
5. Mary Harbage, "The Borrowers at Home and Afield," Elementary English 33 (February 1956): 73.
6. Marcus Crouch and Alex Ellis, eds., *Chosen for Children* (London: Library Association, 1967), 68; hereafter cited in text as Crouch 1967.
7. Mary Norton, Introduction, *The Borrowers Omnibus* (London: J. M. Dent, 1966), ix; hereafter cited in text as *Omnibus.*
8. Ruth Ulman, "WLB Biography: Mary Norton," *Wilson Library Bulletin* 36 (May 1962): 767; hereafter cited in text as Ulman.
9. Doris de Montreville and Donna Hill, eds., *The Third Book of Junior Authors* (New York: H. W. Wilson, 1972), 211; hereafter cited in text as de Montreville.
10. Norah Smaridge, *Famous Modern Storytellers for Young People* (New York: Dodd, Mead, 1969), 80; hereafter cited in text as Smaridge.
11. Cecily Hamilton and Lilian Baylis, *The Old Vic* (London: Jonathan Cape, 1926), 9.
12. Richard Findlater, *Lilian Baylis: The Lady of the Old Vic* (London: Allen Lane, 1975), 17.
13. John Eppstein, *Portugal: The Country and Its People* (London: Queen Anne Press, 1967), 1; hereafter cited in text as Eppstein.
14. Mary Norton, *The Borrowers Afloat* (New York: Harcourt, Brace, 1959), 23; hereafter cited in text as *Afloat.*
15. Edna Johnson, Evelyn R. Sickels, Frances Clarke Sayers, eds., *Anthology of Children's Literature* (New York: Houghton, Mifflin, 1970), 1252; hereafter cited in text as Johnson.
16. Gerard J. Senick, ed., *Children's Literature Review*, vol. 6 (Detroit: Gale Research, 1984), 219; hereafter cited in text as Senick.

17. J. Ethel Wooster, "Children's Books," *Library Journal,* 15 April 1944, 355.

18. Marjorie Fischer, "New Books for the Younger Reader's Library," *New York Times Book Review,* 27 October 1957, 46.

19. *Children's Books: Awards and Prizes* (New York: Children's Book Council, 1981), 131.

20. Mary Norton, *Poor Stainless* (San Diego: Harcourt, Brace, 1971), 31; hereafter cited in text as *Poor.*

21. The spelling of the name of Arrietty's cousin is inexplicably changed from Timmis in *The Borrowers Afloat* to Timmus in *The Borrowers Avenged.*

22. Mary Norton, *The Borrowers Avenged* (San Diego: Harcourt, Brace, 1982), 297; hereafter cited in text as *Avenged.*

Chapter Two

1. Jean de Temple, "The Magic of Mary Norton," *Ontario Library Review* 42 (November 1958): 207.

2. "The Taste for Magic," *Times Literary Supplement,* 15 November 1957, iii.

3. Some recent readers have objected to the stereotyping of the cannibals and the witch doctor in this scene. In light of ethnographic knowledge of the Polynesian Islands, the portrayal is both insulting and demeaning. Norton, however, was creating a caricature of the "savages" of children's adventure novels popular in her youth. The scene itself is so humorously exaggerated in its fantasy that the author cannot have believed or have expected her readers to believe in the reality of the characters presented. An examination of the portrayal of Mild Eye, the gypsy who appears in the Borrowers series, will reveal Norton taking another approach to a popular stereotype of her day.

4. Marcus Crouch, *The Nesbit Tradition: The Children's Novel in England* (Totowa, N.J.: Rowman & Littlefield, 1972), 16, hereafter cited in text as Crouch 1972.

5. E. Nesbit, *The Phoenix and the Carpet.*

6. Mary Croxson, "The Emancipated Child in the Novels of E. Nesbit," *Signal* 14 (May 1974): 56.

7. Mary Cadogan and Patricia Craig, *Woman and Children First: The Fiction of Two World Wars* (London: Victor Gollancz, 1978), 215.

8. Mary Norton, *The Magic Bed-Knob* (London: J. M. Dent, 1945), 7: hereafter cited in text as *Magic.*

9. Linda Hutcheon, *A Theory of Parody: The Teaching of Twentieth Century Art Forms* (New York and London: Methuen, 1985), 36; hereafter cited in text as Hutcheon.

10. P. L. Travers, *Mary Poppins* (New York: Harcourt, Brace, Jovanovich, 1962), 8.

11. Mary Norton, *Bed-Knob and Broomstick* (San Diego: Harcourt, Brace, Jovanovich, 1974), 17; hereafter cited in text as *Bed-Knob.*

12. Kenneth Grahame, *The Golden Age,* illustrated by Ernest Shepard, foreword by Naomi Lewis (London: Bodley Head, 1979), 13.

13. See, for example, Barbara Walker, *The Crone: Woman of Age, Wisdom, and Power* (New York: Harper & Row, 1985); hereafter cited in text as Walker.

14. In discussing the question "Why do we always need more stories?" J. Hillis Miller writes that it may be "because in *some* way they do *not* satisfy. Stories, however perfectly conceived and powerfully written, however moving, do not accomplish successfully their allotted function. Each story and each repetition or variation of it leaves some uncertainty or contains some loose end unraveling its effect. . . . And so we need another story, and then another, and yet another, without ever coming to the end of our need for stories or without ever assuaging the hunger they are meant to satisfy" (J. Hillis Miller, "Narrative," in *Critical Terms for Literary Study,* ed. Frank Lentricchia and Thomas McLaughlin [Chicago: University of Chicago Press, 1990], 72). This statement helps to explain Mary Norton's interest in sequels throughout her writing career. Not only does she write within the fashionable and profitable tradition of "series" children's books, but she also seems to have understood, either consciously or intentionally, the ideas articulated later by Miller. In the Borrowers series, Kate's need to know more about the Clock family and the narrator's suggestion that stories go on and on seem to reflect these ideas.

15. Roderick K. McGillis, "Editor's Comments," *Children's Literature Association Quarterly* 14 (Winter 1989): 162.

16. Some readers see in Miss Price's finding happiness in the past an echo of E. Nesbit's *Harding's Luck,* in which the central character moves to his ancestral home and the seventeenth century. Norton's main point, however, seems to be that Miss Price is a misfit in her twentieth-century village. Nesbit also develops concepts of the circularity of time, ideas that seem to be of little interest to Norton. In the Borrowers series, she presents time as linear; the Clock family is constantly leaving homes behind them forever. In *Are All the Giants Dead?* she is interested in the lives of fairy-tale characters after the conclusions of their most famous exploits. Their pasts exist only in their own minds or in the imaginations of children who remember the stories.

17. Julia Davenport, "The Narrative Framework of *The Borrowers:* Mary Norton and Emily Brontë," *Children's Literature in Education* 49 (Summer 1983): 75; hereafter cited in text as Davenport.

Chapter Three

1. Nigel Hand, "Mary Norton and *The Borrowers,*" *Children's Literature in Education* 7 (March 1972): 38; hereafter cited in text as Hand.

2. Marcus Crouch, "Salute to Children's Literature and Its Creators," in *Readings about Children's Literature,* ed. Evelyn R. Robinson (New York: David McKay, 1966), 185.

3.   Margaret Rustin and Michael Rustin, "Deep Structures of Fantasy in Modern British Children's Books," *The Lion and the Unicorn* 10 (1986): 61; hereafter cited in text as Rustin and Rustin.

4.   Lois Kuznets, "Mary Norton's *The Borrowers:* Diaspora in Miniature," in *Touchstones: Reflections on the Best in Children's Literature,* vol. 1, ed. Perry Nodelman (West Lafayette, Ind.: ChLA Publishers, 1985): 202; hereafter cited in text as Kuznets 1985a.

5.   Annis Pratt, *Archetypal Patterns in Women's Fiction* (Bloomington: Indiana University Press, 1981), 39 ff.; hereafter cited in text as Pratt 1981.

6.   Barbara Hardy, *Tellers and Listeners: The Narrative Imagination* (London: Athlone Press, 1975); hereafter cited in text as Hardy.

7.   Inger Christensen, *The Meaning of Metafiction* (Bergen: Universitets Forlaget, 1981), 11; hereafter cited in text as Christensen.

8.   Mary Norton, *The Borrowers* (London: J. M. Dent, 1952), 7; hereafter cited in text as *Borrowers* English edition 1952.

9.   William Faulkner, *Absalom, Absalom!* (New York: Modern Library, 1951), 11. Anita Moss quotes this passage in "Varieties of Children's Metafiction" (*Studies in the Literary Imagination* 18 [Fall 1985]: 79), although she does not relate it to *The Borrowers.*

10.   Carol Christ, *Diving Deep and Surfacing: Women Writers on Spiritual Quest,* 2d ed. (Boston: Beacon Press, 1986), 1.

11.   See, for example, Cheryl B. Torsney, "The Critical Quilt: Alternative Authority in Feminist Criticism," in *Contemporary Literary Theory,* ed. G. Douglas Atkins and Laura Morrow (Amherst: University of Massachusetts Press, 1989), 180–99.

12.   In "Anatomy of a Masterpiece: *The Borrowers*" (*Language Arts* 53 [May 1976]; 538–44), I have discussed this activity in detail. Lois Kuznets has also noted the symbolic significance in "Permutations of Frame in Mary Norton's 'Borrowers' Series," *Studies in the Literary Imagination* 18 (Fall 1985): 70; hereafter cited in text as Kuznets 1985b.

13.   David Richter, *Fable's End: Completeness and Closure in Rhetorical Fiction* (Chicago: University of Chicago Press, 1974), quoted in Moss, 84.

14.   Wallace Stevens, "The Idea of Order at Key West," in *The Palm at the End of the Mind: Selected Poems and a Play,* ed. Holly Stevens (New York: Vintage, 1972), 98.

15.   Frederick L. Gwynn and Joseph L. Blotner, eds., *Faulkner at the University* (New York: Vintage, 1965), 273–74.

16.   Anne Commire, ed., "Mary Norton 1903–," in *Something about the Author,* vol. 18 (Detroit: Gale Research, 1980), 239; hereafter cited in text as Commire.

17.   Virginia L. Wolf has discussed this aspect of *The Borrowers* in "From the Myth to the Wake of a Home: Literary Houses," *Children's Literature* 18 (1990): 53–67.

Chapter Four

1. Mary Norton, *The Borrowers Aloft* (New York: Harcourt, Brace, Jovanovich, 1961), 32; hereafter cited in text as *Aloft*.

2. Quoted in Annis Pratt, "Spinning among Fields: Jung, Fry, Lévi-Strauss, and Feminist Archetypal Theory," in *Feminist Archetypal Theory: Interdisciplinary Re-visions of Jungian Thought,* ed. Estella Lauter and Carol Schreirer Rupprecht (Knoxville: University of Tennessee Press, 1985), 2.

3. Sheila Egoff, *Worlds Within: Children's Fantasy from the Middle Ages to Today* (Chicago: American Library Association, 1988), 157.

4. It could be objected that Norton presents Mild Eye as a stereotyped character, demeaning the gypsy people frequently found wandering in Europe and England at the end of the nineteenth century; however, Norton is in many ways sympathetic in her portrayal. She sees him as a marginalized individual, surviving through skillful borrowing of what more affluent individuals do not need. His capture of the Clocks is an accidental result of his retrieving his "own" lost property. Through Arrietty's words, Norton expresses sympathy for his unhappy married life with a woman who does not believe him. While it is fortunate that he does not capture the Clocks when they are stranded during the flood, it is an unfortunate irony that he is mistakenly arrested for poaching, an activity he would have been driven to in order to feed himself and his wife.

5. Kate's behavior is not unlike that of the Wilson children at the beginning of *Bonfires and Broomsticks* or that of Curdie early in George MacDonald's *The Princess and Curdie* and Susan during the later books of C. S. Lewis's Chronicles of Narnia. Each of these writers is interested in the loss and then restoration of or failure to restore belief.

6. Mary Norton, *The Borrowers Afield* (London: J. M. Dent, 1955), 5.

7. Bruno Bettelheim, *The Uses of Enchantment: The Meaning and Importance of Fairy Tales* (New York: Alfred A. Knopf, 1976), 225–35.

8. At the end of the first decade of the twentieth century, the *Illustrated London News* contained many articles about the newly popular sport of ballooning (no specific one of which seems to be related directly to Arrietty's reading). Her creative response to her reading, working with her father to adapt the details of this human sport to objects around them and to their own needs, is an example of her growth as a Borrower. This episode offers a parallel to the activity of storytelling: drawing on and combining older materials in a new and vital way.

9. In *Archetypal Patterns*, Pratt suggests that in most adult novels the female does not marry her green-world lover, returning instead into the male-dominated society. Perhaps Norton, writing as she is for children, allows wish fulfillment to take over, making it possible for Arrietty to marry her green-world lover and achieve a happily-ever-after life based on an equal relationship between partners. This relationship would be much different from that experienced by the royal fairy-tale couples depicted in *Are All the Giants Dead?*

10. In her unpublished paper "The Child in the Female Pastoral World: Houses as Images of Nurturance in Early Twentieth-Century Children's Books by Women," Phyllis Bixler discusses such female characters as Mary Lennox (*The Secret Garden*) and Anne Shirley (*Anne of Green Gables*) who open houses to the world of nature and bring objects from nature into the home. This, she suggests, marks an important step in the female characters' maturation processes. Arrietty's free movement through the open grate and her bringing produce into the Clocks' new home could also be seen as another step toward female adulthood.

11. These ideas are explored in detail in Rustin and Rustin ("Deep Structures") and Kuznets ("Permutations").

Chapter 5

1. Mary Norton. *Are All the Giants Dead?* (New York: Harcourt, Brace, Jovanovich, 1975), 13; hereafter cited in text as *Giants*.

2. Sandra Gilead in "Magic Abjured: Closure in Children's Fantasy Fiction" (*PMLA* 106 [March 1991]: 277–93), discusses this type of fantasy pattern, but does not mention *Are All the Giants Dead?*

3. Wolfgang Iser, "The Reading Process: A Phenomenological Approach," in *Reader-Response Criticism: From Formalism to Post-Structuralism*, ed. Jane P. Tompkins (Baltimore and London: Johns Hopkins University Press, 1980), 50–69.

4. Joseph Campbell. *The Hero with a Thousand Faces* (Princeton, N.J.: Princeton University Press, 1949).

Chapter Six

1. T. H. White, *Mistress Masham's Repose* (Boston: Gregg Press, 1980), 34; hereafter cited in text as White.

2. Lucy M. Boston, "A Message from Green Knowe," *Horn Book* 39 (June 1963): 259.

3. Lucy M. Boston, *The Stones of Green Knowe* (Harmondsworth, England: Penguin Books, 1979), 43.

4. Lucy M. Boston, *An Enemy at Green Knowe* (Harmondsworth, England: Penguin Books, 1977), 116.

5. Lucy M. Boston, *The River at Green Knowe* (Harmondsworth, England: Penguin Books, 1976), 108.

6. It is interesting to note that both authors based their stories and situated their symbolic dwellings in locales less than 100 miles apart: Boston in the Huntingdonshire area to which she moved only in middle age, and Norton in the Bedfordshire area in which she spent only her childhood.

7. In many ways, Boston's attitude toward Green Knowe is closest to Kenneth Grahame's attitude toward the River Bank in *Wind in the Willows*, a place successful in resisting onslaughts from outside, even though, as noted, *The*

Borrowers Afield and *The Borrowers Afloat* contain numerous direct parallels to Grahame's work.

8. Gillian Avery, "Mary Norton," in *Twentieth-Century Children's Writers,* 3d ed., ed. Tracy Chevalier (Chicago: St. James Press, 1989), 770.

9. Two notable exceptions are Lucy M. Boston, in her Green Knowe series, and African-American children's author Virginia Hamilton, in a number of novels. The importance of storytelling to the listener is emphasized in the 1992 motion picture *Fried Green Tomatoes.*

10. A useful summary of Barthes's ideas can be found in John Sturrock, *Structuralism and Since: From Lévi-Strauss to Derrida* (New York: Oxford University Press, 1979), 52–80.

Selected Bibliography

PRIMARY WORKS

Are All The Giants Dead? London: Dent, and New York: Harcourt Brace, 1975.
Bed-Knob and Broomstick. London: Dent, and New York: Harcourt Brace, 1957.
Bonfires and Broomsticks. London: Dent, 1947.
The Borrowers. London: Dent, 1952; and New York: Harcourt Brace, 1953.
The Borrowers Afield. London: Dent, and New York: Harcourt Brace, 1955.
The Borrowers Afloat. London: Dent, and New York: Harcourt Brace, 1959.
The Borrowers Aloft. London: Dent, and New York: Harcourt Brace, 1961.
The Borrowers Avenged. London: Kestrel, and New York: Harcourt Brace, 1982.
The Magic Bed-Knob. New York: Hyperion, 1943, and London: Dent, 1945.
Poor Stainless. London: Dent, and New York: Harcourt Brace, 1971.

SECONDARY WORKS

Avery, Gillian. "Mary Norton." In *Twentieth Century Children's Writers,* 3d ed, edited by D. L. Kirkpatrick, 729–30. Chicago: St. James Press, 1989. This short critical overview examines the ways in which Norton has created "a powerful mythology" in the Borrowers series.
Commire, Anne, ed. "Mary Norton, 1903–." In *Something about the Author,* vol. 18, 236–39. Detroit: Gale Research, 1980. Presents chronologically arranged background information, including many of Norton's own statements about her life.
Davenport, Julia. "The Narrative Framework of *The Borrowers:* Mary Norton and Emily Brontë." *Children's Literature in Education* 49 (Summer 1983): 75–79. After outlining relationships between the narrative techniques of *The Borrowers* and *Wuthering Heights,* Davenport suggests that the frame narrations of the two novels provide elements of both credibility and questioning about past, improbable events.
Hand, Nigel. "Mary Norton and *The Borrowers*." *Children's Literature in Education* 7 (March 1972): 38–55. In addition to praising the author's style, Hand analyzes the ways in which the characters' imaginative responses to events influence their senses of fulfillment.

_____. "Mary Norton, Fred Inglis, and the World We Have Lost." In *Good Writers for Children,* edited by Dennis Butts, 86–93. St. Albans, England: Hart-Davis, 1977. In discussing Mary Norton's interest in the role of the imagination, Hand examines her use of that faculty to "recapture the past, whether it be in a positive or negative spirit."

Harbage, Mary. "The Borrowers at Home and Afield." *Elementary English* 33 (February 1956): 67–75. A general appraisal of the first two Borrowers books, followed by summaries of critical responses and of the author's life.

Kuznets, Lois R. "Mary Norton's *The Borrowers:* Diaspora in Miniature." In *Touchstones: Reflections on the Best in Children's Literature,* vol. 1, edited by Perry Nodelman, 198–203. West Lafayette, Ind.: Children's Literature Association, 1985. A discussion of how themes and characterization in the novel are influenced by Norton's attitudes toward social and economic conditions in England and Europe during and after World War II.

_____. "Permutations of Frame in Mary Norton's 'Borrowers' Series." *Studies in the Literary Imagination* 18 (Fall 1985): 65–78. An in-depth analysis of the significance of the narrative frames of the first three books in the series and the implications of these being dropped in the last two.

de Montreville, Doris, and Donna Hill, eds. "Mary Norton." In *The Third Junior Book of Authors,* 211–13. New York: Wilson, 1972. Norton's autobiographical reminiscence of her childhood and the years before her marriage is followed by a brief summary of the events of her life.

Olson, Barbara V. "Mary Norton and the Borrowers." Elementary English 47 (February 1970): 185–89. Discusses the merits of the (at that time apparently) completed series, emphasizing style, themes, and characterization.

Rawson, Claude. "Little People." *London Review of Books,* 15 September 1983, 20–21. A detailed comparison of themes and techniques in the Borrowers series, Swift's *Gulliver's Travels,* and T. H. White's *Mistress Masham's Repose.*

Rees, David. "Freedom and Imprisonment—Mary Norton." In *What Do Draculas Do? Essays on Contemporary Writers of Fiction for Children and Young Adults,* 1–14. Metuchen, N.J., and London: Scarecrow Press, 1990. Argues that the portrayal of events and characters in all of Norton's novels are influenced by this major theme. A brief but perceptive analysis of the body of Norton's work.

Rustin, Michael, and Margaret Rustin. "Deep Structures of Fantasy in Modern British Children's Books." *The Lion and the Unicorn* 10 (1986): 60–82. Argues that the enduring qualities of the Borrowers series are to be found in the deep thematic structures that are made understandable to children through the vivid presentation of the characters, events, and settings of the novels.

_____. "Who Believes in 'Borrowers'?" In *Narratives of Love and Loss,* 163–80. London: Verso, 1987. A condensation of the preceding article, the essay focuses on the theme of "felt deprivation" in both the historical setting of the novels and the times in which they were written.

Senick, Gerard J., ed. "Mary Norton, 1903–." In *Children's Literature Review*, vol. 6, 210–27. Detroit: Gale Research, 1984. Includes excerpts from articles of general commentary about Norton's works, as well as short sections from British and American reviews of her novels.

Smaridge, Norah. "Mary Norton." In *Famous Modern Storytellers for Young People*, 79–85. New York: Dodd, Mead, 1969. Written for younger readers, this chapter provides biographical information, followed by brief summaries and appreciations of Norton's novels.

Stott, Jon C. "Anatomy of a Masterpiece: *The Borrowers*." *Language Arts* 55 (May 1976): 538–44. Argues that the unifying feature of the novel is to be found in the concept of "seeing," and the related ideas of "insight" and "understanding."

Thomas, Margaret. "Discourse of the Difficult Daughter: A Feminist Reading of Mary Norton's *Borrowers*." *Children's Literature in Education* 84 (March 1992): 39–48. Argues that in order to achieve maturity, Arrietty must reshape her life in radical ways, thus escaping the "captivity of her conditioning."

Ulman, Ruth. "WLB Biography: Mary Norton." *Wilson Library Bulletin* 36 (May 1962): 767. A concise but insightful biographical sketch of the author's life up to the publication of *The Borrowers Aloft*.

Wolf, Virginia L. "From the Myth to the Wake of Home: Literary Houses." *Children's Literature* 18 (1990), 53–67. Argues that *The Borrowers*, like many children's novels since the middle of the twentieth century, is "a study of home as a potential bomb rather than a womb."

Index

The Author

Jon C. Stott, Professor of English at the University of Alberta, teaches courses in children's and American literature. A member of the founding board and the first president of the Children's Literature Association, he has also been active in the Children's Literature Assembly. His articles on the study and teaching of children's literature have appeared in Canadian, American, and British periodicals, and he is the author of *Children's Literature from A to Z: A Guide for Parents and Teachers* (1984) and, with Raymond E. Jones, *Canadian Books for Children: A Guide to Authors and Illustrators* (1988) and is coeditor, with Anita Moss, of *The Family of Stories: An Anthology of Children's Literature* (1986).